The paradise of childhood: a manual for self-instruction in Friedrich Froebel's educational principles, and a practical guide to kinder-gartners

Edward Wiebé

THE

PARADISE OF CHILDHOOD:

A MANUAL FOR SELF-INSTRUCTION IN FRIEDRICH FROEBEL'S
EDUCATIONAL PRINCIPLES,

AND A PRACTICAL

Guide to Kinder-Gartners.

BY

EDWARD WIEBÉ.

WITH SEVENTY-FOUR PLATES OF ILLUSTRATIONS.

MILTON BRADLEY & COMPANY,
SPRINGFIELD, MASS.

SPRINGFIELD PRINTING COMPANY,
ELECTROTYPERS, PRINTERS AND BINDERS,
SPRINGFIELD, MASS

INTRODUCTION.

UNTIL a recent period, but little interest has been felt by people in this country, with regard to the Kinder-Garten method of instruction, for the simple reason that a correct knowledge of the system has never been fully promulgated here. However the lectures of Miss E. P. Peabody of Cambridge, Mass, have awakened some degree of enthusiasm upon the subject in different localities, and the establishment of a few Kinder Garten schools has served to call forth a more general inquiry concerning its merits.

We claim that every one who believes in rational education, will become deeply interested in the peculiar features of the work, after having become acquainted with Froebel's principles and plan, and that all that is needed to enlist the popular sentiment in its favor is the establishment of institutions of this kind, in this country, upon the right basis.

With such an object in view, we propose to present an outline of the Kinder Garten plan as developed by its originator in Germany, and to a considerable extent by his followers in France and England.

But as Froebel's is a system which must be carried out faithfully in all its important features, to insure success, we must adopt his plan as a whole and carry it out with such modifications of secondary minutiæ only, as the individual case may acquire without violating its fundamental principles. If this cannot be accomplished, it were better not to attempt the task at all.

The present work is entitled a *Manual for Self Instruction and a Practical Guide for Kinder Gartners.* Those who design to use it for either of these purposes, must not expect to find in it all that they ought to know in order to instruct the young successfully according to Froebel's principles. No book can ever be written which is able to make a perfect Kinder-Gartner; this requires the training of an able teacher actively engaged in the work at the moment. "Kinder Garten Culture," says Miss Peabody, in the preface to her "Moral Culture of Infancy," "is the adult mind entering into the child's world and appreciating nature's intention as displayed in every impulse of spontaneous life, so directing it that the joy of success may be ensured at every step, and artistic things be actually produced which gives the self reliance and conscious intelligence that ought to discriminate human power from blind force."

With this thought constantly present in his mind, the reader will find, in this book, all that is indispensably necessary for him to know, from the first establishment of the Kinder-Garten through all its various degrees of development, including the use of the materials and the engagement in such occupations as are peculiar to the system. There is much more, however, that can be learned only by individual observation. The fact that here and there, persons, presuming upon the slight knowledge which they may have gained of Froebel and his educational principles, from books, have established schools called Kinder-Gartens, which in reality had nothing in common with the legitimate Kinder-Garten but the name, has caused distrust and even opposition, in many minds towards everything that pertains to this method of instruction. In discriminating between the spurious and the real, as is the design of this work, the author would mention with special commendation, the Educational

Institute conducted by Mrs and Miss Kriege in Boston It connects with the Kinder Garten proper, a Training School for ladies, and any one who wishes to be instructed in the correct method, will there be able to acquire the desired knowledge

Besides the Institute just mentioned, there is one in Springfield, Mass, under the supervision of the writer, designed not only for the instruction of classes of children in accordance with these principles, but also for imparting information to those who are desirous to become Kinder Gartners From this source, the method has already been acquired in several in stances, and as one result, it has been introduced into two of the schools connected with the State Institution at Monson, Mass.

The writer was in early life acquainted with Froebel, and his subsequent experience as a teacher has only served to confirm the favorable opinion of the system, which he then derived from a personal knowledge of its inventor A desire to promote the interests of true education, has led him to undertake this work of interpretation and explanation

Without claiming for it perfection, he believes that, as a guide, it will stand favorably in comparison with any publication upon the subject in the English or the French language

The German of Marenholtz, Goldammer, Morgenstern and Froebel have been made use of in its preparation, and though new features have, in rare cases only, been added to the original plan, several changes have been made in minor details, so as to adapt this mode of instruction more readily to the American mind This has been done, however, without omitting aught of that German thoroughness, which characterizes so strongly every feature of Froebel's system

The plates accompanying this work are reprints from "Goldammer's Kinder Garten,"a book recently published in Germany

The Paradise of Childhood:
A GUIDE TO KINDER-GARTNERS.

ESTABLISHMENT OF A KINDER-GARTEN.

THE requisites for the establishment of a "Kinder Garten" are the following

1 A house, containing at least one large room, spacious enough to allow the children, not only to engage in all their occupations, both sitting and standing, but also to practice their movement plays, which, during inclement seasons, must be done in doors

2 Adjoining the large room, one or two smaller rooms for sundry purposes

3 A number of tables, according to the size of the school, each table affording a smooth surface ten feet long and four feet wide, resting on movable frames from eighteen to twenty four inches high The table should be divided into ten equal squares, to accommodate as many pupils, and each square subdivided into smaller squares of one inch, to guide the children in many of their occupations On either side of the tables should be settees with folding seats, or small chairs ten to fifteen inches high The tables and settees should not be fastened to the floor, as they will need to be removed at times to make room for occupations in which they are not used

4 A piano forte for gymnastic and musical exercises—the latter being an important feature of the plan, since all the occupations are interspersed with, and many of them accompanied by, singing

5 Various closets for keeping the apparatus and work of the children—a wardrobe, washstand, chairs, teacher's table, &c

The house should be pleasantly located, removed from the bustle of a thoroughfare, and its rooms arranged with strict regard to hygienic principles A garden should surround or, at least, adjoin the building, for frequent out door exercises, and for gardening purposes A small plot is assigned to each child, in which he sows the seeds and cultivates the plants, receiving, in due time, the flowers or fruits, as the result of his industry and care

When a Training School is connected with the Kinder Garten the children of the "Garten" are divided into groups of five or ten — each group being assisted in its occupations by one of the lady pupils attending the Training School

Should there be a greater number of such assistants than can be conveniently occupied in the Kinder Garten, they may take turns with each other In a Training School of this kind, under the charge of a competent director, ladies are enabled to acquire a thorough and practical knowledge of the system They should bind themselves, however, to remain connected with the institution a specified time, and to follow out the details of the method patiently, if they aim to fit themselves to conduct a Kinder Garten with success

In any establishment of more than twenty children, a nurse should be in constant attendance It should be her duty also to preserve order and cleanliness in the rooms, and to act as janitrix to the institution.

MEANS AND WAYS OF OCCUPATION

IN THE KINDER-GARTEN.

———• • •———

BEFORE entering into a description of the various means of occupation in the Kinder-Garten, it will be proper to state that Friedrich Froebel, the inventor of this system of education, calls *all occupations* in the Kinder-Garten "*plays*," and the materials for occupation "*gifts*" In these systematically arranged plays, Froebel starts from the fundamental idea that all education should begin with a development of the *desire for activity innate in the child*, and he has been, as is universally acknowledged, eminently successful in this part of his important work Each step in the course of training is a logical sequence of the preceding one, and the various means of occupation are developed, one from another, in a perfectly natural order, beginning with the simplest and concluding with the most difficult features in all the varieties of occupation Together, they satisfy *all the demands* of the child's nature in respect both to mental and physical culture, and lay the surest foundation for all subsequent education in school and in life

The *time of occupation* in the Kinder Garten is three or four hours on each week day, usually from 9 to 12 or 1 o'clock, and the time allotted to each separate occupation, including the changes from one to another, is from twenty to thirty minutes *Movement* plays, so called in which the children imitate the flying of birds, swimming of fish, the motions of sowing, mowing, threshing. &c, in connection with light gymnastics and vocal exercises alternate with the plays performed in a sitting posture All occupations that can be engaged in out of doors, are carried on in the garden whenever the season and weather permit

For the reason that the various occupations, as previously stated, are so intimately connected, growing, as it were, out of each other, they are introduced very gradually, so as to afford each child ample time to become sufficiently prepared for the next step, without interfering, however, with the rapid progress of such as are of a more advanced age, or endowed with stronger or better developed faculties

The following is a list of the *gifts* or material and means of occupation in the Kinder-Garten, each of which will be specified and described separately hereafter

There are altogether twenty *gifts*, according to Froebel's general definition of the term, although the first six only are usually designated by this name We choose to follow the classification and nomenclature of the great inventor of the system

LIST OF FROEBEL'S GIFTS

1 Six rubber balls, covered with a net-work of twine or worsted of various colors

2 Sphere, cube, and cylinder, made of wood

3 Large cube, consisting of eight small cubes

4 Large cube, consisting of eight oblong parts

5 Large cube, consisting of whole, half, and quarter tubes

6 Large cube consisting of doubly divided oblongs

[The third, fourth fifth and sixth gifts serve for building purposes]

7 Square and triangular tablets for laying of figures

8 Staffs for laying of figures

9 Whole and half rings for laying of figures

10 Material for drawing

11 Material for perforating.

12. Material for embroidering.

13 Material for cutting of paper and combining pieces.

14 Material for braiding

15 Slats for interlacing

16 The slat with many links

17 Material for intertwining

18 Material for paper folding

19 Material for peas-work

20 Material for modeling

THE FIRST GIFT.

THE First Gift which consists of six rubber balls, over wrought with worsted, for the purpose of representing the three fundamental and three mixed colors, is introduced in this manner

The children are made to stand in one or two rows, with heads erect, and feet upon a given line, or spots marked on the floor The teacher then gives directions like the following

" Lift up your *right* hands as high as you can raise them "

" Take them down "

" Lift up your *left* hands " " Down "

" Lift up both your hands " " Down "

" Stretch forward your right hands, that I may give each of you something that I have in my box "

The teacher then places a ball in the hand of each child, and asks—

" Who can tell me the name of what you have received?" Questions may follow about the *color, material, shape,* and other qualities of the ball, which will call forth the replies, *blue, yellow rubber, round light, soft,* &c

The children are then required to repeat sentences pronounced by the teacher, as— ' The *ball* is *round,* " " *My ball* is *green,* " " *All* these balls are made of *rubber,*" &c They are then required to return all, except the *blue* balls, those who give up theirs being allowed to select from the box a *blue* ball in

exchange, so that in the end each child has a ball of that color The teacher then says " Each of you has now a *blue, rubber ball* which is *round soft,* and *light,* and these balls will be your balls to play with. I will give you another ball to-morrow and the next day another, and so on, until you have quite a number of balls, all of which will be of *rubber,* but no two of the same color "

The six differently colored balls are to be used, one on each day of the week, which assists the children in recollecting the days of the week, and the colors After distributing the balls, the same questions may be asked as at the beginning and the children taught to raise and drop their hands with the balls in them , and if there is time they may make a few attempts to throw and catch the balls This is enough for the first lesson , and it will be sure to awaken enthusiasm and delight in the children

The object of the first occupation is to teach the children to distinguish between the *right* and the *left* hand and to name the various colors It may serve also to develop their vocal organs, and instruct them in the rules of politeness How the latter may be accomplished, even with such simple occupation as playing with balls, may be seen from the following

In presenting the balls, pains should be taken to make each child extend the right hand, and do it gracefully The teacher, in putting the ball into the little outstretched hand, says

"Charles, I place this red (green, yellow, &c,) ball into your right hand" The child is taught to reply—

"I thank you, sir"

After the play is over, and the balls are to be replaced, each one says, in returning his ball—

"I place this red (green, yellow, &c) ball, with my right hand, into the box"

When the children have acquired some knowledge of the different colors they may be asked at the commencement

"With which ball would you like to play this morning—the green, red, or blue one?" The child will reply

"With the blue one, if you please," or one of such other color as may be preferred

It may appear rather monotonous to some to have each child repeat the same phrase, but it is only by constant repetition and patient drill that anything can be learned accurately, and it is certainly important that these youthful minds in their formative state, should be taught at once the beauty of order and the necessity of rules So the *left* hand should never be employed when the *right* hand is required, and all mistakes should be carefully noticed and corrected by the teacher One important feature of this system is the inculcation of habits of precision

The children's knowledge of color may be improved by asking them what other things are similar to the different balls, in respect to color After naming several objects they may be made to repeat sentences like the following

"My ball is green, like a leaf" "My ball is yellow, like a lemon" "And mine is red, like blood," &c

Whatever is pronounced in these conversational lessons should be articulated very distinctly and accurately, so as to develop the organs of speech, and to correct any defect of utterance, whether constitutional or the

result of neglect Opportunities for phonetic and elocutionary practice are here afforded Let no one consider the infant period as too early for such exercises If children learn to *speak* well before they learn to *read*, they never need special instruction in the art of reading with expression

For a second play with the balls, the class forms a circle, after the children have received the balls in the usual manner They need to stand far enough apart, so that each, with arms extended can just touch his neighbor's hand Standing in this position, and having the balls in their right hands the children pass them into the left hands of their neighbors In this way each one gives and receives a ball at the same time, and the left hands should, therefore, be held in such a manner that the balls can be readily placed in them The arms are then raised over the head, and the balls passed from the left into the right hand, and the arms again extended into the first position This process is repeated until the balls make the complete circuit, and return into the right hands of the original owners The balls are then passed to the left in the same way, everything being done in an opposite direction This exercise should be continued until it can be done rapidly and, at the same time gracefully

Simple as this performance may appear to those who have never tried it, it is, nevertheless, not easily done by very young children without frequent mistakes and interruptions It is better that the children should not turn their heads so as to watch their hands during the changes, but be guided solely by the sense of touch, and to accomplish this with more certainty, they may be required to close their eyes It is advisable not to introduce this play or any of the following until expertness is acquired in the first and simpler form

In the third play the children form in two rows fronting each other Those of one row only receive balls These they toss to the opposite row first one by one, then two by two, finally the whole row at once, always to the counting of the teacher—"one, two, throw'

Again, forming four rows, the children in the first row toss up and catch, then throw to the second row, then to the third, then to the fourth, accompanying the exercise with counting as before, or with *singing*, as soon as this can be done

For a further variety, the balls are thrown upon the floor, and caught, as they rebound, with the *right* hand or the *left* hand, or with the hand inverted or they may be sent back to the floor several times before catching

Throwing the balls against the wall, tossing them into the air, and many other exercises may be introduced whenever the balls are used, and will always serve to interest the children Care should be taken to have every movement performed in perfect order, and that every child take part in all the exercises in its turn

At the close of every ball play, the children occupy their original places marked on the floor, the balls are collected by one or two of the older pupils, and after this has been done, each child takes the hand of its opposite neighbor, and bowing, says, " good morning," when they march by twos, accompanied by music, once or twice through the hall, and then to their seats for other occupation

THE SECOND GIFT.

THE Second Gift consists of a *sphere*, a *cube*, and a *cylinder* These the teacher places upon the table, together with a rubber ball, and asks

" Which of these three objects looks most like the ball ? "

The children will certainly point out the sphere but of course, without giving its name

' Of what is it made?" the teacher asks, placing it in the hand of some pupil or rolling it across the table

The answer will doubtless be, " Of wood " " So we might call the object a *wooden ball* But we will give it another name We will call it a *sphere* "

Each child must here be taught to pronounce the word, enunciating each sound very distinctly The ball and sphere are then further compared with each other as to material, color, weight, &c, to find their similarities and dissimilarities Both are *round*, both *roll* The ball is *soft*, the sphere is *hard*. The ball is *light*, the sphere is *heavy* The sphere makes a *louder* noise when it falls from the table than the ball The ball rebounds when it is thrown upon the floor, the sphere does not All these answers are drawn out from the pupils by suitable experiments and questions, and every one is required to repeat each sentence when fully explained

The children then form a circle, and the teacher rolls the sphere to one of them, asking the child to stop it with both his feet This child then takes his place in the center, and rolls the sphere to another one, who again stops it with his feet, and so on, until all the children have in turn taken their place in the center of the circle At another time, the children may sit in two rows upon the floor, facing each other A white and a black sphere are then given to the heads of the rows, who exchange by rolling them across to each other Then the spheres are rolled across obliquely to the second individuals in the rows These exchange as before, and then roll the spheres to those who sit third, and so on until they have passed throughout the lines and back again to the head Both spheres should be rolling at the same instant, which can be effected only by counting or when time is kept to accompanying music

Another variety of play in the use of this gift consists in placing the rubber ball at a distance on the floor, and letting each child, in turn, attempt to hit it with the sphere

For the purpose of further instruction, the sphere, cube, and cylinder are again placed upon the table, and the children are asked to discover and designate the points of resemblance and difference in the first two They will find, on examination, that both are made of wood, and of the same color, but the sphere can roll, while the cube cannot Inquire the cause for this difference, and the answer will, most likely, be either, " the sphere is round," or " the cube has corners "

" How many corners has the cube? ' The children count them, and reply, " Eight."

If I put my finger on one of these corners, and let it glide down to the corner below it, (thus,) my finger has passed along an *edge* of the cube How many such edges can we count on this cube? I will let my finger glide over the edges, one after the other, and you may count "

"One, two, three, —————— — — — 12 "

"Our cube, then, has eight corners, and twelve edges I will now show you four corners and four edges, and say that this part of the cube, which is contained between these four corners and four edges, is called a *side* of the cube Count how many sides the cube has "

" One two, three, four, five, six '

" Are these sides all alike, or is one small and another large? " " They are all alike "

' Then we may say that our cube has six sides, all alike, and that each side has four edges, all alike Each of these sides of the cube is called a *square* "

To explain the cylinder, a conversation like the following may take place It will be observed that instruction is here given mainly by comparison, which is, in fact, the only philosophical method

The sphere, cube, and cylinder are placed together as before, in the presence of the children They readily recognize and name the first two, but are in doubt about the third whether it is a barrel or a wheel They may be suffered to indulge their fancy for awhile in finding a name for it, but are, at last told that it is a *cylinder*, and are taught to pronounce the word distinctly and accurately

" What do you see on the cylinder which you also see on the cube? " " The cylinder has two sides " " Are the sides square, like those of the cube? " " They are not "

But the cylinder can *stand* on these sides just as the cube can Let us see if it cannot *roll*, too, as the sphere does Yes ! it rolls, but not like the sphere, for it can roll only in two ways, while the sphere can roll any way So you see, the sphere, cube, and cylinder are alike in some respects, and different in others Can you tell me in what respects they are just alike? "

" They are made of wood, are smooth, are of the same color, are heavy, make a loud noise when they fall on the floor "

These answers must be drawn out by experiments with the objects and by questions, logically put, so as to lead to these results as natural conclusions The exercise may be continued, if desirable by asking the children to name objects which look like the sphere, cube, or cylinder The edge of a cube may also be explained as representing a *straight line* The point where two or three lines or edges meet is called a *corner*, the inner point of a corner is an *angle*, of which each side, or square, of the cube has four To sum up what has already been taught The cube has six sides, or squares, all alike, eight corners, and twelve edges, and each side of the cube has four edges, all alike, four corners, and four angles

The sphere, cube, and cylinder, when suspended by a double thread, can be made to rotate around themselves, for the purpose of showing that the sphere appears the same in form in whatever manner we look at it, that the cube when rotating, (suspended at the center of one of its sides,) shows the form of the cylinder, and that the cylinder, when rotating, (suspended at the center of its round side,) presents the appearance of a sphere

Thus, there is, as it were, an inner triunity in these three objects—sphere contained in cylinder, and cylinder in cube, the cylinder forming the mediation between the two others, or the transition from one to the other. Although the child may not be told, the teacher may think, in this connection, of the natural law, according to which the fruit is contained in the flower, the flower is hidden in the bud

Suspended at other points, cylinder and cube present other forms, all of which are interesting for the children to look at, and can be made instructive to their young minds, if accompanied by apt conversation on the part of the teacher

THE THIRD GIFT.

THIS consists of a *cube*, divided into *eight smaller one inch cubes*

A prominent desire in the mind of every child is to *divide* things, in order to examine the parts of which they consist. This natural instinct is observable at a very early period. The little one tries to change its toy by breaking it, desirous of looking at its inside, and is sadly disappointed in finding itself incapable of reconstructing the fragments. Froebel's Third Gift is founded on this observation. In it the child receives a *whole*, whose *parts* he can easily *separate*, and *put together again at pleasure*. Thus he is able to do that which he could not in the case of the toys—restore to its original form that which was broken—making a perfect whole. And not only this—he can use the parts also for the construction of other *wholes*

The child's first plaything, or means of occupation, was the *ball*. Next came the *sphere*, similar to, yet so different from, the ball. Then followed *cube* and *cylinder*, both, in some points, resembling the sphere, yet each having its own peculiarities, which distinguish it from the sphere and ball. The pupil, in receiving the cube, divisible into eight smaller cubes, meets with friends, and is delighted at the multiplicity of the gift. Each of the eight parts is precisely like the whole, except in point of size, and the child is immediately struck with this quality of his first toy for *building purposes*. By simply looking at this gift, the pupil receives the ideas of *whole* and *part*—of *form* and *comparative size*, and by dividing the cube, is impressed with the relation of one part to another in regard to position and order of movements, thus learning readily to comprehend the use of such terms as *above, below, before, behind, right, left*, &c, &c

With this and all the following gifts, we produce what Froebel calls *forms of life, forms of knowledge* and *forms of beauty*

The first are representations of objects which actually *exist*, and which come under our common observation, as the works of human skill and art. The second are such as afford instruction relative to *number, order, proportion*, &c. The third are figures representing only *ideal forms*, yet so regularly constructed as to present perfect models of *symmetry* and *order* in the arrangement of the parts. Thus in the occupations connected with the use of these simple building blocks, the child is led into the living world—there first to take notice of objects by comparison, then to learn something of their properties by induction, and lastly, to gather into his soul a love and desire for the beautiful by the contemplation of those forms which are regular and symmetrical

THE PRESENTATION OF THE THIRD GIFT

The children having taken their usual seats, the teacher addresses them as follows

"To-day, we have something new to play with"

Opening the package and displaying the box, he does not at once gratify their curiosity by showing them what it contains, but commences by asking the question—

"Which one of the three objects we played with yesterday does this box look like?"

They answer readily, "The cube"

"Describe the box as the cube has been described, with regard to its sides, edges, corners, &c"

If this is satisfactorily done, the cover may then be removed, and the box placed inverted upon the table   If the box is made of wood, it is placed upon its cover, which, when drawn out will allow the cubes to stand on the table Lifting it up carefully, so that the contents may remain entire, the teacher asks

"What do you see now?"

The answer is as before, "A cube"

One of the scholars is told to push it across the table   In so doing, the parts will be likely to become separated, and that which was previously whole will lie before them in fragments   The children are permitted to examine the small cubes, and after each one of them has had one in his hand, the eight cubes are returned to the teacher, who remarks

"Children as we have broken the thing, we must try to *mend* it   Let us see if we can put it together as it was before"

This having been done, the boxes are then distributed among the children, and they are practiced in removing the covers, and taking out the cube without destroying its unity They will find it difficult at first, and there will be many failures   But let them continue to try until some, at least, have succeeded, and then proceed to another occupation.

PREPARATION FOR CONSTRUCTING FORMS

The surface of the tables is covered with a net work of lines, forming squares of one inch The spaces allotted to the pupils are separated from each other by heavy dark lines, and the centers are marked by some different color In these first conversational lessons, the children must be taught to point out the right upper corner of their table space, the left upper the right and left lower, the upper and lower edges, the right and left edges, and the center   With little staffs or sticks cut at convenient lengths, they may indicate direction, e g , by laying them upon the table in a line from left to right, covering the center of the space, or extending them from the right upper to the left lower corner covering the center, then from the middle of the upper edge to the middle of the lower edge, and so on   The teacher must be careful to use terms that can be easily comprehended, and avoid changing them in such a way as to produce any ambiguity in the mind of the child

Here, as in the more advanced exercises, everything should be done with a great deal of precision   The children must understand that order and regularity in all the performances are of the utmost importance   The following will serve as an illustration of the method   The children having received the boxes, they are required to place them exactly in the center of their spaces, so as to cover four squares.   They then take hold of the box with the left hand, and remove the cover with the right, placing it by the right upper corner of the net-work on the table   They next place the left hand upon the open box, and reverse it with the right hand, so that the left is on the table   Drawing it carefully from beneath, they let the inverted box rest on the squares in the center   The right hand is used to raise the box carefully from its place, and, if successful, eight small cubes will stand in the center of the space, forming one large cube   Lastly, the box is placed in the cover at the right upper corner, and care should be taken that all are arranged in exact position

(If the cubes are enclosed in wooden boxes with covers to be drawn out at the side, these manipulations are to be changed accordingly)

At the close of any play, when the materials are to be returned to the teacher, the same minuteness of detail must be observed

Replacing the box over the cubes placing the left hand beneath, and lifting the box with the right, reversing it, and placing it again upon the center of the table, then covering it—these are processes which must be re peated many times before the scholar can acquire such expertness as shall render it desirable to proceed to the real building occupation

FORMS OF LIFE

The boxes being opened as directed, and the cubes upon the center squares—in each space—the question is asked

"How many little cubes are there?"
"Eight"

' Count them, placing them in a row from left to right," (or from right to left)

"What is that?" "A row of cubes"

It may bear any appropriate name which the children give it—as "a train of cars," "a company of soldiers," "a fence," &c.

"Now count your cubes once more, placing them one upon another What have you there?"

"An upright row of eight cubes"

"Have you ever seen anything standing like this upright row of cubes?"

"A chimney" "A steeple"

"Take down your cubes and build two upright rows of them — one square apart What have you now?"

"Two little steeples," or "two chimneys" Thus, with these eight cubes, many forms of life can be built under the guidance of the teacher It is an important rule in this occupation, that nothing should be rudely destroyed which has been constructed, but each new form is to be produced by slight change of the preceding one

On Plates I and II , a number of these are given They are designated by Froebel as follows

1 Cube, or Kitchen Table
2 Fire-Place
3 Grandpa's Chair
4 Grandpa's and Grandma's Chairs
5 A Castle, with two towers
6 A Stronghold
7 A Wall
8. A High Wall
9. Two Columns
10 A Large Column, with two memorial stones
11 Sign-Post
12 Cross
13 Two Crosses
14 Cross, with pedestal
15 Monument
16 Sentry-Box
17 A Well
18 City Gate
19 Triumphal Arch
20. City Gate, with Tower.
21 Church
22 City Hall
23 Castle
24. A Locomotive
25 A Ruin
26 Bridge, with Keeper's House
27 Two Rows of Trees
28 Two Long Logs of Wood
29. A Bole
30 Two Small Logs of Wood
31 Four Garden Benches
32 Stairs
33 Double Ladder.
34 Two Columns on Pedestals
35 Well-Trough.
36 Bath
37 A Tunnel
38 Easy Chair
39 Bench, with back.
40. Cube

Several of the names in this list represent objects which, being more specifically German, will not be recognized by the children Ruins, castles, sentry-boxes, sign-posts, perhaps they have never seen, but it is easy to tell them something about these objects which will interest them   They will listen with pleasure to short stories, narrated by way of explanation, and thus associating the story with the form, be able, at another time to reconstruct the latter while they repeat the former in their own words   It is not to be expected, however, that teachers in this country should adhere closely to the list of Froebel   They may, with advantage vary the forms, and, if they choose affix other names to those given upon the plates   It is well sometimes to adopt such designations as are suggested by the children themselves   They will be found to be quite apt in tracing resemblances between their structures and the objects with which they are familiar.

In order to make the occupation still more useful, they should be required also to point out the dissimilarities existing between the form and that which it represents

It is proper to allow the child, at times, to *invent* forms, the teacher assisting the fantasy of the little builder in the work of constructing, and in assigning names to the structure. When a figure has been found, and named, the child should be required to take the blocks apart, and build the same several times in succession   Older and more advanced scholars suggest to younger and less abler ones, and the latter will be found to appreciate such help

It is a common observation, that the younger children in a family develop more rapidly than the older ones, since the former are assisted in their mental growth by companionship with the latter.   This benefit of association is seen more fully in the Kinder Garten, under the judicious guidance of a teacher who knows now to encourage what is right, and check what is wrong, in the disposition of the children

It should be remarked, in connection with these directions, that in the use of this and the succeeding gift it is essential that *all* the blocks should be used in the building of each figure, in order to accustom the child to look upon things as mutually related   There is nothing which has not its appointed place. and each part is needed to constitute the whole   For example, the well-trough (35) may be built of six cubes, but the remaining two should represent two pails with which the water is conveyed to the trough

FORMS OF KNOWLEDGE

These do not represent objects, either real or ideal.   They instruct the pupil concerning the properties and relations of numbers, by a particular arranging and grouping of the blocks   Strictly speaking, the first effort to count, by laying them on the table one after another, is to be classed under this head. The form thus produced, though varied at each trial, is one of the forms of knowledge, and by it the child receives its first lesson in arithmetic.

Proceeding further, he is taught to add, always by using the cubes to illustrate the successive steps   Thus, having placed two of the blocks at a little distance from each other on the table, he is caused to repeat, " One and one are two "   Then placing another upon the table, he repeats, " One and two are three," and so on, until all the blocks are added

Subtraction is taught in a similar manner   Having placed all the cubes upon the table. the scholar commences taking them off, one at a time, repeating, as he does this, " One from eight leaves seven, ' One from seven leaves six " and so on

According to circumstances, of which the Kinder Gartner, of course, will be the best judge these exercises may be continued further by adding and subtracting two, three, and so on ; but care should always be taken that no new step be made until all that has gone before is perfectly understood

With the more advanced classes, exercises in multiplication and division may be tried, by grouping the blocks

The division of the large cube, to illustrate the principles of proportion, is an interesting and instructive occupation; and we will here proceed to give the method in detail.

The children have their cube of eight before them on the table. The teacher is also furnished with one, and lifting the upper half in the manner shown on Plate I., No. 4, asks:

"Did I take the whole of my cube in my hand, or did I leave some of it on the table?"

"You left some on the table."

"Do I hold in my hand more of my cube than I left on the table, or are both parts alike?"

"Both are alike."

"If things are alike, we call them *equal*. So I divided my cube into two equal parts, and each of these equal parts I call a *half*. Where are the two halves of my cube?"

"One is in your hand; the other is on the table."

"So I have two *half* cubes. I will now place the half which I have in my hand upon the half standing on the table. What have I now?"

"A whole cube."

The teacher, then separating the cube again into halves, by drawing four of the smaller cubes to the right and four to the left, as is indicated on Plate I., No. 2, asks:

"What have I now before me?"

"Two half cubes."

"Before, I had an upper and a lower half. Now, I have a right and a left half. Uniting the halves again I have once more a whole."

The scholars are taught to repeat as follows, while the teacher divides and unites the cubes in both ways, and also as represented by Form No. 3:

"One whole—two halves."

"Two halves—one whole."

Again, *each half* is divided, as shown in Forms No. 5, 6, and 7, and the children are required to repeat during these occupations:

"One whole—two halves."

"One half—two quarters (or fourths)."

"Two quarters—one half."

"Two halves—one whole."

After these processes are fully explained, and the principles well understood by the scholars, they are to try their hand at dividing of the cube—first, individually then all together. If they succeed, they may then be taught to separate it into eighths. It is not advisable, in all cases, to proceed thus far.

Children under four years of age should be restricted, for the most part, to the use of the cubes for practical building purposes, and for simpler forms of knowledge.

FORMS OF BEAUTY.

Starting with a few simple arrangements, or positions, of the blocks, we are able to develop the forms contained in this class by means of a fixed law, viz., that every change of position is to be accompanied by a corresponding movement on the opposite side. In this way symmetrical figures are constructed in infinite variety, representing no real objects, yet, by their regularity of outline, adapted to please the eye, and minister to a correct artistic taste. The love of the beautiful cannot fail to be awakened in the youthful mind by such an occupation as this, and with this emotion will be associated, to some extent, the love of the good, for they are inseparable.

The works of God are characterized by perfect order and symmetry, and his goodness is commensurate with the beauty manifest everywhere in the fruits of his creative power. The construction of forms of beauty with the building blocks will prepare the child to appreciate, by and by, the order that rules the universe.

By Plates IV. and V. it will be seen that these forms are of only one block's height, and, consequently, represent outlines of surfaces. It is necessary that the children should be guided, in their construction, by an easily recognizable center. Around this visible point all the separate parts of the form to be created must be arranged, just as in working out the highest destiny of man, all his thoughts and acts need to be regulated by an invisible center, around which he is to construct a harmonious and beautiful whole

In order to produce the varied forms of beauty with the simple material placed in the hands of the scholar, he must first learn in what ways two cubes may be brought in contact with each other. Four positions are shown on Plate IV. The blocks may be arranged either—side by side, as in Fig 1 , edge to edge, as in Fig 2 , or edge to side and side to edge, as in Nos 3 and 4 Nos 1 and 3 are the opposites to 2 and 4 Other changes of position may be made For example, in Fig 1 the block marked *a* may be placed above or to the right or to the left of the block marked *b* The cubes may also be placed in certain relations to each other on the table, without being in actual contact These positions should be practiced perseveringly at the outset, so as to furnish a foundation for the processes of construction which are to follow It is one of the important features of Froebel's system, that it enables the child readily to discover, and critically to observe, all relations which objects sustain to one another Thoroughness, therefore, is required in all the details of these occupations

We start from any fundamental form that may present itself to our mind Take, for illustration, Form No 5 Four cubes are here united side to side, constituting a square surface, and the outline is completed by placing the four remaining cubes severally side to side with this middle square In 6, edge touches edge , in 7, side touches edge, and in

8, edge touches side midway. Another mode of development is shown in Forms 9—15

The four outside cubes move toward the right by a half cube's length, until the original form reappears in No 15

Now, the four outside cubes occupy the *opposite* position Fig 16, edges touch sides They are moved as before, by a half cube's length, until, in Form No 22, the one with which we started, is regained.

We now extract the inside cubes (*b*), Fig 23 and each of them travels around its neighbor cube (*a*), until a standing, hollow square is developed, as in Fig. 29

Now cube *a* again is set in motion It assumes a slanting direction to the remaining cubes, Fig 30, and, pursuing its course around them, the Form, No 29, reappears in No 36

Next, *b* is drawn out Fig 37 and *a* pushed in, until a standing cross is formed, Fig 38 *b*, constantly traveling on by a half cube's length, until, Fig 43 all cubes are united in a large square, and *b* again begins traveling by a cube's length, turning side to side and edge to edge. In Fig 48, *b* performs as *a* has done

But with more developed children we may proceed on other principles, Fig 49, introducing changes only on two instead of four sides, and thus arriving successively at Forms 50—60

After each occupation the scholars should replace their cubes in the boxes as heretofore described and the material should be returned to the closet where it is kept before commencing any other play

THE FOURTH GIFT.

THE preceding gift consisted of cubical blocks, all of their three dimensions being the same. In the Fourth Gift, we have greater variety for purposes of construction, since each of the parts of the large cube is an oblong, whose length is twice its width, and four times its thickness. The dimensions bear the same proportion to each other as those of an ordinary brick; and hence these blocks are sometimes called bricks. They are useful in teaching the child difference in regard to length, breadth, and height. This difference enables them to construct a greater variety of forms than he could by means of the third gift. By these he is made to understand, more distinctly, the meaning of the terms perpendicular and horizontal. And if the teacher sees fit to pursue the course of experiment sufficiently far, many philosophical truths will be developed; as, for instance, the law of equilibrium, shown by laying one block across another, or the phenomenon of continuous motion, exhibited in the movement of a row of the blocks, set on end, and gently pushed from one direction.

PREPARATION FOR CONSTRUCTING FORMS.

This gift is introduced to the children in a manner similar to the presentation of the third gift. The cover is removed, and the box is reversed upon the table. Lifting the box carefully, the cube remains entire. The children are made to observe that, when whole, its size is the same as that of the previous one. Its parts, however, are very different in form, though their number is the same. There are still eight blocks. Let the scholars compare one of the small cubes of the third gift with one of the oblongs in this gift; note the simi-

larities and the differences; then, if they can comprehend that notwithstanding they are so unlike in *form*, their *solid contents* is the same, since it takes just eight of each to make the same sized cube, an important lesson will have been learned. If told to name objects that resemble the oblong, they will readily designate a *brick, table, piano, closet*, &c., and if allowed to invent forms of life, will, doubtless, construct *boxes, benches*, &c.

The same precision should be observed in all the details of opening and closing the plays with this gift as in those previously described.

FORMS OF LIFE.

The following is a list of Froebel's forms, which are represented on Plates VI. and VII. If the names do not appear quite striking, or to the point, the teacher may try to substitute better ones:

1. The Cube.
2. Part of a Floor, or Top of a Table.
3. Two Large Boards.
4. Four Small Boards.
5. Eight Building Blocks.
6. A Long Garden Wall.
7. A City Gate.
8. Another City Gate.
9. A Bee Stand.
10. A Colonnade.
11. A Passage.
12. Bell Tower.
13. Open Garden House.
14. Garden House, with Doors.
15. Shaft.
16. Shaft.
17. A Well, with Cover.
18. Fountain.
19. Closed Garden Wall.

20 An Open Garden
21 An Open Garden •
22 Watering-Trough
23. Shooting-Stand
24. Village
25 Triumphal Arch
26 Caroussel
27 Writing Desk
28 Double Settee
29 Sofa
30 Large Garden Settee
31. Two Chairs
32 Garden Table Chairs
33 Children's Table
34 Tombstone
35 Tombstone
36 Tombstone
37. Monument
38 Monument
39 Winding Stairs
40 Broader Stairs
41 Stalls
42 A Cross Road
43 Tunnel
44 Pyramid
45 Shooting-Stand
46 Front of a House
47 Chair, with Footstool.
48 A Throne
49. ⎰ Illustration of
50 ⎱ Continuous Motion

Here, as in the use of the previous gift, one form is produced from another by slight changes, accompanied by explanations on the part of the teacher   Thus, Form 30 is easily changed to 31, 32, and 33 and Form 34 may be changed to 35, 36, and 37   In every case, all the blocks are to be employed in constructing a figure

FORMS OF KNOWLEDGE

This gift like the preceding, is used to communicate ideas of divisibility Here, however, on account of the particular form of the parts, the processes are adapted rather to illustrate the division of a surface, than of a solid body

The cube is first arranged so that one perpendicular and three horizontal cuts appear, and a child is then requested to separate it into halves, these halves into quarters, and these quarters into eighths   Each of the latter will be found to be one of the oblong blocks, and this for the time, may be made the subject of conversation

"Of what material is this block made?"
'What is the color?"
"What objects resemble it in form?"
"How many sides has it?"
"Which is the largest side?"
'Which is the smallest side?"
"Is there a side larger than the smallest and smaller than the largest?"

In this way, the scholars learn that there are three kinds of sides, symmetrically arranged in pairs   The upper and lower, the right and left, the front and back, are respectively equal to and like each other

By questions, or by direct explanation, facts like the following, may be made apparent to the minds of children   "The upper and lower sides of the block are twice as large as the two long sides, or the front and back as they may be called   Again, the front and back are twice as large as the right and left, or the two short sides of the block   Consequently, the two largest sides are four times as large as the two smallest sides " ⸳This can be demonstrated in a very interesting way, by placing several of the blocks side by side, in a variety of positions   and in all these operations the children should be allowed to experiment for themselves   The small cubes of the preceding gift may also with propriety be brought in comparison with the oblongs of this gift and the differences observed

When the single block has been employed to advantage through several lessons, the whole cube may then be made use of, for the representation of forms of knowledge

Construct a tablet or plane as in Plate VIII a   In order to show the relations of dimension, divide this plane into halves either by a perpendicular or horizontal cut (b and c)

These two forms will give rise to instruct-ive observations and remarks by asking

" What was the form of the original tablet?"

"What is the form of its halves?"

" How many times larger is their breadth than their height?"

So with regard to the position of the oblong halves, the one at *b* may be said to be *lying* while that at *c* is *standing*

" Change a lying to a standing oblong " In order to do this, the child will move the first so as to describe a quarter of a circle to the right or left

" Unite two oblongs by joining their small sides You then have a large lying oblong"(*e*)

"Separate again (*f*) and divide each part into halves, (*i*) You have now four parts called quarters, and these are squares, in their surface form "

Each of these quarters may be subdivided, and the children taught the method of division by two Other material may also be used in connection with the blocks, such as apples, or any small objects which serve to illustrate the properties of number It is evident that these operations should be conducted in the most natural way, and never begun at too early a stage of development of the little ones In figures *c*, *g h* and *k* on Plate VIII another mode is indicated, for the purpose of illus-trating further the conditions of form connect-ed with this gift Figs *1*—16 Plate VIII show the manner in which exercises in addition and subtraction may be introduced, as has al-ready been alluded to in the description of the Third Gift

FORMS OF BEAUTY.

We first ascertain, as in the case of the cubes, the various modes in which the oblongs can be brought in relation to each other These are much more numerous than in the Third Gift, because of the greater variety in

the dimensions of the parts Plate IX shows a number of forms of beauty derivable from the original form, I Each two blocks form a separate group, which four groups touching in the center, form a large square The out side blocks (*a*) move in Figs. 1—9, around the stationary middle

The inside blocks (*b*) are now drawn out (Fig 10), then the blocks (*a*) united to form a hollow square (Fig 11), around which *b* moves gradually (Figs 12 and 13).

Now *b* is combined into a cross with open center, *a* goes out (Fig 14) and moves in an opposite direction until Fig 17 appears

By extricating *b* the eight rayed star (Fig 18) is formed. In Fig. 19 *a* revolves, *b* is drawn out until edge touches edge, and thus the form of a flower appears (Fig 20)

Now *b* is turned (Fig 21), and in Fig 22, a wreath is shown In Fig 22, the inside edges touch each other, in Fig 23, inside and outside, in Fig 24, edges with sides, and *b* is united to a large hollow square, around which *a* commences a regular moving In Fig 29, *a* is finally united to a lying cross, and thereby another starting-point gained for a new series of developments

Each of these figures can be subjected to a variety of changes by simply placing the blocks on their long or short sides, or as the children will say, by letting them *stand up* or *lie down* The net-work of lines on the table is to be the constant guide, in the con-struction of forms In inventing a new series. place a block above, below, at the right or left of the center, and a second opposite and equidistant A third and a fourth are placed at the right and left of these. but in the same position relative to the center The remain ing four are placed symmetrically about those first laid. By moving the *a*'s or *b*'s regularly in either direction, a variety of figures may be formed.

THE FIFTH GIFT

CUBE, TWICE DIVIDED IN EACH DIRECTION.

(PLATES X TO XVI)

———•♦•———

ALL gifts used as occupation material in the Kinder-Garten develop, as previously stated, one from another The Fifth Gift, like that of the Third and Fourth Gifts, consists of a cube again, although larger than the previous ones The cube of the Third Gift was divided *once* in all directions The natural progress from 1 is to 2 , hence the cube of the Fifth Gift is divided *twice* in all directions , consequently in *three equal parts*, each consisting of *nine* smaller cubes of *equal size* But as this division would only have multiplied, not diversified the occupation material, it was necessary to introduce a new element by subdividing some of the cubes in a slanting direction

We have heretofore introduced only perpendicular and horizontal lines These opposites, however, require their mediate element, and this mediation was already indicated in the forms of life and of beauty of the Third and Fourth Gifts, when side and edge, or edge and side, were brought to touch each other The slanting direction appearing there transitionally—occasionally—here, becomes permanent by introducing the slanting line, separated by the division of the body, as a bodily reality

Three of the part cubes of the Fifth Gift are divided into half cubes, three others into quarter cubes, so that there are left twenty-one whole cubes of the twenty-seven, produced by the division of the cube mentioned before, and the whole Gift consists of thirty-nine single pieces

It is most convenient to pack them in the box, so as to have all half and quarter cubes and three whole cubes in the bottom row, (see Plate XV , 1ˣ) which only admits of separating the whole cube in the various ways required hereafter, as it will also assist in placing the cube upon the table, which is done in the same manner as described with the previous Gifts

The first practice with this Gift is like that with others introduced thus far. Led by the question of the teacher, the pupils state that this cube is larger than their other cubes , and the manner in which it is divided will next attract their attention They state how many times the cube is divided in each direction, how many parts we have if we separate it according to these various divisions and carrying out what we say, gives them the necessary assistance for answering these questions correctly In No 3, Plate XV , the three parts of the cube have been laid side by side of each other

These three squares we can again divide in three parts, and these latter again in three, so that then we shall have twenty-seven parts, which teaches the pupil that $3 \times 3 = 9$ $3 \times 9 = 27$

To some the repetition of the apparently simple exercises may appear superfluous , but repetition alone, in this simple manner, will assist children to remember, and it is always interesting, as they have not to deal with abstractions, but have real things to look at for the formation of their conclusions

4

But, again I say, do not continue these occupations any longer than you can command the attention of your pupils by them. As soon as signs of fatigue or lack of interest become manifest, drop the subject at once, and leave the Gift to the pupils for their own amusement. If you act according to this advice, your pupils never will over exert themselves, and will always come with enlivened interest to the same occupation whenever it is again taken up.

After the children have become acquainted with the manner of division of their new large cube, and have exercised with it in the above-mentioned way, their attention is drawn to the shape of the divided half and quarter cubes.

They are divided by means of *slanting lines*, which should be made particularly prominent, and the pupils are then asked to point out, on the whole cubes, in what manner they were divided in order to form half and quarter cubes. The pupils also point out horizontal, perpendicular and slanting lines which they observe in things in the room or other near objects.

Take the two halves of your cube apart, and say, " How many corners and angles you can count on the upper and lower sides of these two half cubes?" " Three." Three corners and three angles, which latter, you recollect, are the insides of corners. We call, therefore, the upper and lower side of the half cube a triangle, which simply means a side or plane with *three* angles. The child has now enriched its knowledge of lines by the introduction of the oblique or slanting line, in addition to the horizontal and perpendicular lines, and of sides or planes by the introduction of the triangle, in addition to the square and oblong previously introduced. With the introduction of the triangle, a great treasure for the development of forms is added, on account of its frequent occurrence as elementary forms in all the many formations of regular objects.

The child is expected to know this Gift now

sufficiently to employ it for the production of the various forms of life and beauty now to be introduced.

FORMS OF LIFE
(PLATES X AND XI)

The main condition here, as always, is that for each representation the whole of the occupation material be employed, not that only one object should always be built, but in such manner that remaining pieces be always used to represent accessory parts, although apart from, yet in a certain relation to the main figure. The child should, again and again, be reminded that nothing belonging to a whole is, or could be, allowed to be superfluous, but that each individual part is destined to fill its position actively and effectively in its relation to some greater whole.

Nor should it be forgotten that nothing should be destroyed, but everything produced by re building. It is advisable always to start with the figure of the cube.

There are only the few following models on our Plates 10 and 11.

1 Cube
2 Flower stand
3 Large Chair
4 Easy Chair, with Foot Bench.
5. A Bed. Lowest row, fifteen whole cubes; second row, six whole and six half cubes, composed of twelve quarter cubes; third row, six half cubes.
6 Sofa. First row, sixteen whole and two half cubes; 6*, ground plan.
7. A Well. 7*, ground plan.
8 House, with Yard. 8*, ground plan; twelve whole cubes, ground; nine whole and six half cubes, second row; roof, twelve quarter cubes.
9 A Peasant's House. First row, ten whole cubes; second row, eight whole and two half cubes; roof, eight cubes, three halves and two halves, and eight quarters and two halves and four quarters; 9*, ground plan.

10 School-House Third row, three whole and six half cubes, fourth row, one whole and four quarter cubes, 10ª, ground plan

11 Church Building itself. eighteen whole cubes, roof, twelve quarter cubes, steeple, four whole cubes and one half cube, vestry, one whole and one half cube, 11ª, ground plan of Church

12 Church, with Two Steeples Building itself, twelve whole cubes, roof, twelve quarter cubes, steeples, twice five whole cubes and one half cube, between steeples, one whole cube, 12ª, ground plan

13 Factory, with Chimney and Boiler-house Factory sixteen whole cubes, roof, six half and four quarter cubes, chimney, five whole and two quarter cubes, boiler-house, four quarter cubes, roof, two quarter cubes, 13ª, ground plan

14 Chapel, with Hermitage

15 Two Garden Houses, with Rows of Trees

16 A Castle 16ª, ground plan

17 Cloister in Ruins 17ª, ground plan

18 City Gate, with Three Entrances 18ª, ground plan

19 Arsenal 19ª, ground plan

20. City Gate, with Two Guard-Houses 20ª, ground plan

21 A Monument 21ª, ground plan, first row, nine whole and four half cubes, second to fourth row, each, four whole cubes, on either side, two quarter cubes, united to a square column, and to unite the four columns, four quarter cubes

22 A Monument 22ª, ground plan, first row, nine whole and four quarter cubes, second row, five whole and four half cubes, third row, four whole cubes, fourth row, four half cubes

23 A Large Cross 23ª, ground plan, first row, nine whole and four times three quarter cubes, second row, four whole cubes, third row, four half cubes

Tables, chairs, sofas, beds, are the first objects the child builds They are the objects with which it is most familiar Then the child builds a house, in which it lives, speaking of kitchen, sleeping room, parlor, and eating room, when representing it Soon the realm of its ideas widens It roves into garden, street, &c It builds the church, the school house, where the older brothers and sisters are instructed, the factory, arsenal, from which, at noon and after the day's work is over, so many laborers walk out to their homes, to eat their dinner and supper, to rest from their work, and to play with their little children The ideas which the children receive of all these objects by this occupation, grow more correct by studying them in their details, where they meet with them in reality In all this they are, as a matter of course, to be assisted by the instructive conversation of the teacher It is not to be forgotten that the teacher may influence the minds of the children very favorably, by relating short stories about things and persons in connection with the object represented. Not their minds alone are to be disciplined, their hearts are to be developed, and each beautiful and noble feeling encouraged and strengthened

Be it remembered again that it is not necessary that the teacher should always follow the course of development shown in the pictures on our plates Every course is acceptable, if only destruction is prevented and re-building adhered to Some of the pictures may not be familiar to some of the children The one has never seen a castle or a city gate, a well or a monument Short descriptive stories about such objects will introduce the child into a new sphere of ideas, and stimulate the desire to see and hear more and more, thus adding, daily and hourly, to the stock of knowledge of which he is already possessed Thus, these plays will not only cultivate the manual dexterity of the child, develop his eye, excite his fantasy, strengthen his power of invention, but the accompanying oral illustrations will also instruct him, and create in him a love for the good, the noble, the beautiful

The Fifth Gift is used with children from five to six years old, who are expected to be in their third year in the Kinder Garten

A box, with its contents, stands on the table before each child They empty the box, as heretofore described, so that the bottom row of the cube, containing the half and quarter cubes, is made the top row

' What have you now ?"

"A cube "

"We will build a church Take off all quarter and half cubes, and place them on the table before you in good order Move the three whole cubes of the upper row together, so that they are all to the left of the other cubes Take three more whole cubes from the right side, and put them beside the three cubes which were left of the upper row Take the three remaining cubes, which were on the right side, and add them to the quarter and half cubes What have you now ? "

"A house without roof, three cubes high, three cubes long, and two cubes broad "

"We will now make the roof Place on each of the six upper cubes a quarter cube with its largest side Fill up the space between each two quarter cubes with another quarter cube, and place another quarter cube on top of it What have you now ?"

" A house with roof"

" How many cubes are yet remaining? '

" Three whole and six half cubes "

" Take the whole cubes, and place them, one on top of the other, before the house Add another cube, made of two half cubes, and cover the top with half a cube for a roof What have you now ?"

" " A steeple "

' We will employ the remaining three half cubes to build the entrance Take two of the half cubes, form a whole cube of them, and place it on the other side of the house, opposite the steeple, and lay upon it the last half cube as a roof What have we built now ?"

" A church, with steeple and entrance "

FORMS OF BEAUTY

If we consider that the Fifth Gift is put into the hands of pupils when they have reached the fifth year, with whom, consequently, if they have been treated rationally, the external organs, the limbs, as well as the senses, and the bodily mediators of all mental activity, the nerves, and their central organ, the brain, have reached a higher degree of development and their physical powers have kept pace with such development, we may well expect a somewhat more extensive activity of the pupils so prepared, and be justified in presenting to them work requiring more skill and ingenuity than that of the previous Gifts

And, in fact, the progress with these forms is apparently much greater than with the forms of life, because here the importance of each of the thirty-nine parts of the cube can be made more prominent He who is not a stranger in mathematics knows that the number of combinations and permutations of thirty nine different bodies does not count by hundreds, nor can be expressed by thousands, but that millions hardly suffice to exhaust all possible combinations

Limitations are, therefore, necessary here , and these limitations are presented to us in the laws of beauty, according to which the whole structure is not only to be formed harmoniously in itself, but each main part of it must also answer the claims of symmetry In order to comply with these conditions, it is sometimes necessary, during the process of building a Form of Beauty, to perform certain movements with various parts simultaneously In such cases it appears advisable to divide the activity in its single parts and allow the child's eye to rest on these transition figures, that it may become perfectly conscious of all changes and phases during the process of development of the form in question This will render more intelligible to the young mind, that real beauty can only be produced when one opposite balances another, if the proportions of all parts are equally regulated by uniting them with one common center

Another limitation we find in the fact, that each fundamental form from which we start is divided in two main parts—the internal and the external—and that if we begin the changes or mutations with one of these opposites, they are to be continued with it until a certain aim be reached   By this process certain small series of building steps are created, which enable the child—and, still more, the teacher—to control the method according to which the perfect form is reached

"Each definite beginning conditions a certain process of its own, and however much liberty in regard to changes may be allowed, they are always to be introduced within certain limits only"

Thus, the fundamental form conditions all the changes of the whole following series. All fundamental forms are distinct from each other by their different centers, which may be a square, (Plate XII, Fig 9,) a triangle, (Plate XIV, Fig 37,) a hexagon, octagon, or circle

Before the real formation of figures commences, the child should become acquainted with the combinations in which the new forms of the divided cubes can be brought with each other   It takes two half cubes, forms of them a whole, and, being guided by the law of opposites, arrives at the forms represented on Plate XII —1 to 8, and perhaps at others of less significance

The series of figures on Plates XIII, XIV, XV, are all developed, one from another, as the careful observer will easily detect   As it would lead too far to show the gradual growing of one from another, and all from a common fundamental form, we will show only the course of development of Figures 9 to 14, on Plate XII

The fundamental form (Fig 9) is a standing square, formed of nine cubes, and surrounded by four equilateral triangles

The course of development starts from the center part   The four cubes a move exter-

nally, (Fig 10,) the four cubes b do the same, (Fig 11,) cubes a move farther to the corner of the triangles, (Fig 12,) cubes b move to the places where cubes a were previously, (Fig 13)   If all eight cubes continue their way in the same manner, we next obtain a form in which a and b remain with their corners on the half of the catheti, then follows a figure like 13, different only in so far as a and b have exchanged positions, then, in like manner, follow 12, 11, 10, and 9.

We, therefore, discontinue the course   The internal cubes so far occupied positions that b and c turned corners, a and c sides towards each other   In Fig 14, the opposite appears, b and c show each other sides, a and c corners   Thus, in Fig 15, we reach a new fundamental form   Here, not the cubes of the internal, but those of the external triangles furnish the material for changing the form

It is not necessary that the teacher, by strictly adhering to the law of development, return to the adopted fundamental form   She may interrupt the course, as we have done, and continue according to new conditions But however useful it may be to leave free scope to the child's own fantasy, we should never lose sight of Froebel's principle, to lead to *lawful action*, to accustom to following a definite rule   Nor should we ever forget that the child can only derive benefit from its occupation, if we do not over-tax the measure of its strength and ability   The laws of formation should, therefore, always be as definite and distinct as simple   As soon as the child cannot trace back the way in which you have led it, in developing any of the forms of life or beauty, if it cannot discover how it arrived at a certain point, or how to proceed from it, the moment has arrived when the occupation not only ceases to be useful, but commences to be hurtful, and we should always studiously avoid that moment

In order to facilitate the child's control of his activity, it is well to give the cubes, which are, so to say, the representatives of the law of development, instead of the letters *a*, *b c*, names of some children present, or of friends of the pupils This enlivens the interest in their movements, and the children follow them with much more attention

FORMS OF KNOWLEDGE
(PLATES XV AND XVI)

The representations of the forms of knowledge, to which the Fifth Gift offers opportunity, is of great advantage for the development of the child To superficial observers, it is true it may appear as if Froebel not only ascribed too much importance to the mathematical element to the disadvantage of others, but that mathematics necessarily require a greater maturity of understanding than could be found with children of the Kinder-Garten age But who thinks of introducing mathematics as a science? Many a child, five or six years of age, has heard that the moon revolves around the earth, that a locomotive is propelled by steam, and that lightning is the effect of electricity These astronomical, dynamic and physical facts have been presented to him, as mathematical facts are presented to his observation in Froebel's Gifts Most assuredly it would be folly, if one would introduce in the Kinder-Garten mathematical problems in the usual abstract manner In the Kinder Garten, the child beholds the bodily representation of an expressed truth, recognizes the same, receives it without difficulty, without overtaxing its developing mind in any manner whatsoever Whatever would be difficult for the child to derive from the mere word, nay, which might under certain circumstances be hurtful to the young mind, is taught naturally and in an easy manner by the forms of knowledge, which thus become the best means of exercising the child's power of observation, reasoning, and judging Beware of all problems and abstractions The child builds, forms, sees, observes, compares, and then expresses the truth it has ascertained By repetition, these truths, acquired by the observation of facts,

become the child's mental property, and this is not to be done hurriedly, but during the last two years in the Kinder Garten and afterwards in the Primary Department

The first seven forms of knowledge on Plate XV show the regular divisions of the cube in three, nine and twenty-seven parts In either case, a whole cube was employed, and yet the forms produced by division are different. This shows that the contents may be equal, when forms are different (Figs 2, 3, 4, or 5 and 6)

This difference becomes still more obvious if the three parts of Fig 2, are united to a standing oblong or those of Fig 3 to a lying oblong, or if a single long beam is formed of Fig 4

Take a cube, children, place it before you, and also a cube divided in two halves, and place the two halves with their triangular planes or sides, one upon another

These two halves united are just as large as the whole cube.

But the two halves may be united also, in other ways They may touch each other with their quadratic and right angular planes

Represent these different ways of uniting the two halves of the cube simultaneously Notwithstanding the difference in the forms, the contents of mass of matter remained the same

In a still more multiform manner, this fact may be illustrated with the cubes divided in four parts Similar exercises follow now with the whole Gift, and the children are led to find out all possible divisions in two, three, four, five, nine and twelve equal parts (Figs 8 to 18)

After each such division the equal parts are to be placed one upon another, for dividing and separating are always to be followed by a process of combining and re uniting The child thus receives every time, a transformation of the whole cube, representing the same amount of matter in various forms (Fig 19–22) The child should also be allowed to compare with each other the various thirds, quarters, or sixths, into which whole cubes can be divided, as shown in Figs 9, 10, 11, 12, or 14, 15 and 16.

It is understood that all these exercises should be accompanied by the living word of the teacher, for thereby, only, will the child become perfectly conscious of the ideas received from perception, and the opportunity is offered to perfect and multiply them The teacher should, however, be careful not to speak too much, for it is only necessary to keep the attention of the pupil to the object represented, and to render impressions more vivid

The divisions introduced heretofore, are followed by representations of regular mathematical figures, (planes,) as shown in Figs 23–26 The manner in which one is formed from the preceding one is easily seen from the figures themselves

As mentioned before, part of the occupation described in the preceding pages, is to be introduced in the Primary Department only, where it is combined with other interesting but more complicated exercises Simply to indicate how advantageously this Gift may be used for instruction in geometry in later years, we have added the Figs 30ª and 30ᵇ, the representation of which shows the child the visible proof of the well known Pythagorean axiom, by which the theoretical abstract solution of the same, certainly, can alone be facilitated

For the continuation of the exercises in arithmetic, begun with the previous Gifts, the cubes of the present one are of great use Exercises in addition and subtraction are continued more extensively, and by the use of these means, the child will be enabled to learn, what is usually called the multiplication table, in a much shorter time and in a much more rational way than it could ever be accomplished by mere memorizing, without visible objects

THE SIXTH GIFT.

LARGE CUBE, CONSISTING OF DOUBLY DIVIDED OBLONGS.

(PLATES XVII TO XX)

As the Third and Fifth Gifts form an especial sequence of development, so the Fourth and Sixth are intimately connected with each other The latter is, so to say, a higher potence of the former, permitting, the observation in greater clearness, of the qualities, relations, and laws, introduced previously

The Gift contains twenty-seven oblong blocks or bricks, of the same dimensions as those of the Fourth Gift Of these twenty-seven blocks eighteen are whole, six are divided breadthwise, each in two squares, and three by a lengthwise cut, each in two columns, altogether making thirty-six pieces

The children soon become acquainted with this Gift, as the variety of forms is much less than in the preceding one, where, by an oblique division of the cubes, an entirely new radical principle was introduced

It is here, therefore, mainly the proportions of size of the oblongs, squares, and columns contained in this Gift and the number of each kind of these bodies, about which the child has to become enlightened before engaging in building—playing, creating—with this new material

The cube is placed upon the table—all parts are disjoined—then equal parts collected into groups, and the child is then asked, "How many blocks have you altogether?" How many oblongs? how many squares? how many columns? Compare the sides of the blocks with another—take an oblong—how many squares do you need to cover it? how many columns?

Place the oblong upon its long edge now upon its shortest side—and state how many squares or columns you need in order to reach its height, in either case Exercises of this kind will instruct the child sufficiently, to allow it to proceed, in a short time. to the individual creating, or producing occupation with this new Gift

FORMS OF LIFE
(PLATES XVII AND XVIII)

It is the forms of life, particularly, for which this Gift provides material, far better fitted, than any previously used The oblongs admit of a much larger extension of the plane. and allow the enclosure of a much more extensive hollow space than was possible. for instance, with the cubes of the Fifth Gift Innumerable forms can therefore be produced with this Gift, and the attention and interest of the pupil will be constantly increased

This very variety, however, should induce the careful teacher to prevent the child's purely accidental production of forms It is always necessary to act according to certain rules and laws, to reach a certain aim The established principle, that one form should always be derived from another, can be carried out here only with great difficulty, owing to the peculiarity of the material It is therefore frequently necessary, particularly with the more complicated structures, to lay an entirely new foundation for the building to be erected

It is necessary. at all times, to follow the child in his operations.—his questions should always be answered and suggestions made to enlarge the circle of ideas

It affords an abundance of pleasure to a child to observe that we understand it and its work, it is, therefore, a great mistake in education to neglect to enter fully into the spirit of the pupil's sphere of thinking and acting, and if we ever should allow ourselves to go so far as to ridicule his productions, instead of assisting him to improve or them, we would certainly commit a most fatal error

The selections of forms of life on Plates XVII and XVIII, nearly all of which are in the meantime forms of art and knowledge, because of their architectural fundamental forms, and the mathematical proportions of their single parts, can, therefore, not fail to give nourishment to various powers of the mind

1 House without roof, back wall has no door 1^a, ground plan

2 Colonnade lowest row, five oblongs laid lengthwise, and back wall consisting of ten standing oblongs, upon which ten squares 2^a, ground plan

3 Hall, with columns

4 Summer House 4^a, ground plan, vestibule formed by six columns

5 Memorial Column of the Three Friends 5^a, ground plan

6 Monument in Honor of Some Fallen Hero. 6^a, ground plan, lowest row, eight oblongs, second square of nine squares, partially constructed of oblongs, third, four single squares, then four columns, four single squares, square of nine squares, square of four squares etc

7 Façade of a Large House 7^a, ground plan.

8 The Columns of the Three Heroes 8^a, ground plan

9 Entrance to Hall of Fame 9^a, ground plan, first row, six squares and six oblongs, second row, six oblongs, third row, six squares, etc

10 Two Story House, with yard 10^a, ground plan 10^b, side view

11 Façade 11^a, ground plan

12 Covered Summer House 12^a, ground plan

13 Front View of a Factory   13ᵃ, ground
plan   13ᵇ, side view
14 Double Colonnade   14ᵃ, ground plan
15 An Altar   15ᵃ, ground plan
16 Monument   16ᵃ, ground plan
17 Columns of Concord   17ᵃ, ground
plan

The fantasy of the child is inexhaustibly rich in inventing new forms   It creates gardens, yards, stables with horses and cattle, household furniture of all kinds, beds with sleeping brothers and sisters in them tables, chairs sofas, etc, etc

If several children combine their individual building they produce large structures, perfect barn-yards with all out-buildings in them, nay, whole villages and towns   The ideas that in union there is strength, and that by co-operation great things may be accomplished, will thus early become manifest to the young mind

FORMS OF BEAUTY
(PLATES XIX. AND XX)

The forms of beauty of this Gift offer far less diversity than those of Gift No 5 , owing, however, to the peculiar proportions of the plane, they present sufficient opportunity for characteristic representations, not to be neglected.

We give on the accompanying plates a single succession of development of such forms The progressive changes are easily recognized, as the oblong, which needs to be moved to produce the following figure, is always marked by a letter.   The center-piece always consists of two of the little columns, standing one upon another, and important modifica-

tions may be produced by using the oblongs in lying or standing positions   By employing the four little columns in various ways, many pleasant changes can be produced by them

FORMS OF KNOWLEDGE.
(PLATE XX)

These also appear in much smaller numbers compared with the richness and multiplicity of the Fifth Gift   By the absence of oblique (obtuse and acute) angles, they are limited to the square and oblong, and exercises introduced with these previously, may be repeated here with advantage

All Froebel's Gifts are remarkable for the peculiar feature that they can be rendered exceedingly instructive by frequently introducing repetitions under varied conditions and forms, by which means we are sure to avoid that dry and fatiguing monotony which must needs result from repeating the same thing in the same manner and form   And still more, the child, thereby, becomes accustomed to recognize like in unlike, similarity in dissimilarity, oneness in multiplicity, and connection in the apparently disconnected

In Fig 16-22, all squares that can be formed with the Sixth Gift are represented In Fig 23 we see a transition from the forms of knowledge to those of beauty.

With the Sixth Gift we reach the end of the two series of development given by Froebel in the building blocks, whose aim is to acquaint the child with the general qualities of the solid body by own observation and occupation with the same.

THE SEVENTH GIFT.

SQUARE AND TRIANGULAR TABLETS FOR LAYING OF FIGURES

(PLATES XXI TO XXIX)

————— •◦•—————

ALL mental development begins with concrete beings The material world with its multiplicity of manifestations first attracts the senses and excites them to activity, thus causing the rudimental operations of the mental powers Gradually—only after many processes, little defined and explained by any science as yet, have taken place—man becomes enabled to proceed to higher mental activity, from the original impressions made upon his senses by the various surroundings in the material world

The earliest impressions, it is true, if often repeated, leave behind them a lasting trace on the mind But between this attained possibility to recall once-made observations, to represent the object perceived by our senses, by mental image (imagination), and the real thinking or reasoning, the real pure abstraction, there is a very long step, and nothing in our whole system of education is more worthy of consideration than the sudden and abrupt transition from a life in the concrete, to a life of more or less abstract thinking to which our children are submitted when entering school from the parental house

Froebel, by a long series of occupation material, has successfully bridged over this chasm which the child has to traverse, and the first place among it, the laying tablets of various forms occupy

The series of tablets is contained in five boxes containing—

A Quadrangular square tablets.

B Right angular (equal sides) ⎫
C Equilateral ⎬ Triangular
D. Obtuse angular (equal sides) ⎪ tablets
E Right angular (unequal sides) ⎭

The child was heretofore engaged with solid bodies, and in the representation of real things It produced a house, garden, sofa, etc. It is true the sofa was not a sofa as it is seen in reality, the one built by the child was, therefore, so to say, an image already, but it was a bodily image, so much so that the child could place upon it a little something representing its doll The child considered it a real sofa, and so it was to the child, fulfilling, as it did, in its little world, the purposes of a real sofa in real life

With the tablets, the embodied planes, the child can not represent a sofa, but a form similar to it, an image of the sofa can be produced by arranging the squares and triangles in a certain order

We shall see, at some future time how Froebel continues on this road, progressing from the plane to the line, from the line to the point and finally enables the child to draw the image of the object, with pencil or pen in his own little hand

A THE QUADRANGULAR LAYING TAB-LETS (SQUARES).

(PLATE XXI)

They are given the child first to the number of six In a similar way as was done with the various building gifts, the child is led to an acquaintance with the various qualities of the new material, and to compare it, with other things, possessing similar qualities It is advisable to let the child understand the connection existing between this and the previous gifts The laying tablets are nothing but the embodied planes, or separated sides of the cube Cover all the sides of a cube with square tablets and after the child has recognized the cube in the body thus formed, let it separate the tablets one by one, from the cube hidden by them

The following, or similar questions are here to be introduced —What is the form of this tablet? How many sides has it? How many angles? Look carefully at the sides Are they alike or unlike each other? They are all alike Now look at the corners These also are all alike Where have you seen similar figures?

What are such figures called? Can you show me angles somewhere else? Where the two walls meet is an angle Here, there, and everywhere you find angles

But all angles are not alike, and they are therefore differently named All these different names you will learn successively, but now let us turn to our tablet Place it right straight before you upon the table Can you tell me now what direction these two sides have which form the angle? The one is horizontal, the other perpendicular An angle which is formed if a perpendicular meets a horizontal line, is called a right angle How many of such angles can you count on your tablet? Four Show me such right angles somewhere else

By the acquisition of this knowledge the child has made an important step forward Looking for horizontal and perpendicular lines, and for right angles, it is led to investigate more deeply the relations of form, which it had heretofore observed only in regard to the size conditioned by it

The child's attention should be drawn to the fact that, however the tablet may be placed the angles always remain right angles though the lines are horizontal and perpen-

dicular only in four positions of the tablet, namely, those where the edges of the tablet are placed in the same direction with the lines on the table before the child This will give occasion to lead the child to a general perception of the standing or hanging of objects according to the plummet

But the tablet will force still another observation upon the child The opposite sides have an equal direction, they are the same distance from each other in all their points, they never meet, however many tablets the child may add to each other to form the lines

The child learns that such lines are called parallel lines It has observed such lines frequently before this, but begins just now to understand their real being and meaning It looks now with much more interest than ever before at surrounding tables, chairs, closets, houses, with their straight line ornaments, for now the little cosmopolitan does not only receive the impressions made by the surroundings upon his senses, but he already looks for something in them, an idea of which lives in his mind Although unconscious of the fact that with the right angle and the parallel line, he received the elements of architecture, it will pleasantly incite him to new observations whenever he finds them again in another object which attracts his attention

The teacher in remembrance of our oft repeated hints, will proceed slowly, and carefully, according to the desire and need of the child She repeats, explains, leads the child to make the same observations in the most different objects, and changing circumstances, or guides the child in laying other forms of knowledge (lying or standing parallelograms Fig 4 and 5) of life, (steps, Fig 6 and 8, double steps, Fig 7 and 9, door, Fig 10. sofa, Fig. 11, cross, Fig 12), or forms of beauty

The number of these forms is on the whole only very limited It is well now to augment the number of tablets in the hands of the pupil, by two when a much larger number of forms can be produced The various series

of forms of beauty, introduced with the third
Gift, can be repeated here and enlarged upon,
according to the change in the material now
at the disposal of the child

B RIGHT-ANGLED TRIANGLES.
(PLATE XXI)

As from the whole cube, the divided cube
was produced, so by division the triangle
springs from the square By dividing it
diagonally in halves, we produce the rectan
gular triangle with equal sides

Although the form of the triangle was presented to the child in connection with the
Fifth Gift, it here appears more independently,
and it is not only on that account necessary
to acquaint the child with the qualities and
being of the new addition to its occupation
material, but still more so as the forms of
the triangles with which, as a natural sequence
it will have to do hereafter, were entirely
unknown to the pupil The child places two
triangles, joined to a square, upon the table

What kind of a line divides your four-cor
nered tablet? An oblique or slanting line.
In what direction does the line cut your
square in two? From the right upper corner
to the left lower corner Such a line we call
a diagonal.

Separate the two parts of the square, and
look at each one separately What do you
call each of these parts? What did you call
the whole? A square How many corners
or angles had the square? Four. How many
corners or angles has the half of the square
you are looking at? Three. This half,
therefore, is called a triangle, because, as I
have explained to you before, it has three
angles. How many sides has your triangle? etc

Looking at the sides more attentively,
what do you observe? One side is long, the
other two are shorter, and like each other
These latter are as large as the sides of the
square, all sides of which were alike

Now tell me what kind of angle it is, that
is formed by these two equal sides? It is a

right angle. Why? and what will you call
the other two angles? How do the sides
run which form these two angles? They run
in such a way as to form a very sharp point,
and these angles are, therefore, called acute
angles, which means sharp pointed angles.
Your triangle has then, how many different
kinds of angles? Two, one right angle, and
two acute angles

It is not necessary to mention that the
above is not to be taught in one lesson It
should be presented in various conversations,
lest the acquired knowledge might not be
retained by even the brightest child The
attention of the pupil may also be led, in
subsequent conversations to the fact that the
largest side is opposite the largest angle, and
that the two acute angles are alike, etc
Sufficient opportunity for these and additional
remarks will offer itself during the representations of forms of life, of knowledge, and of
beauty, for which the child will employ its
tablets, according to its own free will, and
which are not necessarily to be separated,
neither here nor in any other part of these
occupations, although it is well to observe a
certain order at any time

Whenever it can be done, elementary knowl
edge may well be imparted, together with the
representations of forms of life, and forms of
beauty.

In order to invent, the child must have
observed the various positions which a triangle may occupy It will find these acting
according to the laws of opposites, already
familiar to the child

The *right angle*, to the *right below*, (Fig 17)
it will bring into the opposite direction to the
left above, (Fig 18) then into the mediative
positions to the *left below*, (Fig. 19) and to
the *right above*, (Fig 20) By turning it
comes *above* the long side, (Hypothenuse, Fig
21) then opposite *below* it, (Fig 22) then to
the *right*, (Fig 23) and finally to the *left* of
it, (Fig 24).

The various positions of two triangles are
easily found by moving one of them around

the other   Fig 26–31 are produced from
Fig 25, by moving the triangle marked *a*,
always keeping it in its original position,
around the other triangle

In Figs 32–37, the changes are produced,
alternating regularly between a turn and a
move of the triangle *a* In Figs 38–47,
simply turning takes place

After the child has become acquainted with
the first elements from which its formations
develop, it receives for a beginning four of
the triangled tablets.   It then places the
right angles together, and thereby forms a
standing full square, (Fig 48)   .

By placing the tablets in an opposite position, turning the right angles from within to
without, it produces a lying square with the
hollow in the middle, (Fig 49) This hollow
space has the same shape and dimensions as
Fig 48 The child will fancy Fig 48 into the
place of this hollow space, and will thereby
transfer the idea of a full square upon an
empty or hollow one, and will consequently
make the first step from the perception of the
concrete to its idea, the abstraction

The child will now easily find mediative
forms between these two opposites It places
two right angles within and two without,
(Fig 58 and 59) two above, and two below,
(Fig 50) two to the right, and two to the left,
(Fig 51)

So far, two tablets always remained connected with one another By separating
them we produce the new mediative forms,
52, 53, 54 and 55, in which again two and
two are opposites But instead of the right,
the acute angles may meet in a point also,
and thus Figs 56 and 57 are produced,
which are called rotation forms, because the
isolated position of the right angle suggests,
as it were, an inclination to fall, or turn, or
rotate.

The mediation between these two opposite figures is given in Figs 50 and 51—
between them and Figs 49 and 50 in Figs
58 and 59 , and it should be remarked in
this connection, that these opposites are con-

5

ditioned by the position of the right angle in
all these cases

All these exercises accustom the pupil to a
methodic handling of all his material They
develop a correct use of his eye, because
regular figures will only be produced when
his tablets are placed correctly and exactly
in their places shown by the net work on the
table The precaution which must be exercised by the child not to disturb the easily
movable tablets, and the care employed to
keep each in its place, are of the greatest
importance for future necessary dexterity of
hand In a still greater degree than by these
simple elementary forms just described, this
will be the case, when the pupil comes into
possession of the following boxes, containing
a larger number—up to sixty four—tablets for
the formation of more complicated figures,
according to the free exercise of his fantasy

FORMS OF LIFE
(PLATE XXIII)

All hints given in connection with the building blocks, are also to be followed here, with
this difference only, that we produce now
images of objects, whereas, heretofore, we
united the objects themselves.

The child here begins—

A, WITH FOUR TABLETS

And forms with them—
1. A flower-pot   2 A little garden-house
3 A pigeon house

B, WITH EIGHT TABLETS

4 A cottage   5 A canoe or boat   6
A covered goblet   7 A light house   8 A
clock

C, WITH SIXTEEN TABLETS

9 A bridge with two spans   10 A large
gate 11 A church 12 A gate with bel-
fry   13 A fruit basket

D, WITH THIRTY TWO TABLETS

14 A peasant's house   15 A forge with
high chimney 16 A coffee-mill 17 A cof-
fee-pot without handle

18 A two story house   19 Entrance to a railroad depot   20 A steamboat

In No 21, we see the result of combined activity of many children   Although to some grown persons it may appear as if the images produced do not bear much resemblance to what they are intended to represent, it should be remembered that in most cases, the children themselves have given the names to the representations   Instructive conversation should also prevent this *drawing with planes*, as it were, from being a mere mechanical pastime, the entertaining, living word must infuse soul into the activity of the hand and its creations   Each representation, then, will speak to the child and each object in the world of nature and art will have a story to tell to the child in a language for which it will be well prepared

We need not indicate how these conversations should be carried on, or what they should contain   Who would not think, in connection with the pigeon house, of the beautiful white birds themselves and the nest they build, the white eggs they lay, the tender young pigeons coming from them, and the care with which the old ones treat the young ones, until they are able to take care of themselves   An application of these relations to those between parents and children, and, perhaps those between God and man, who, as his children enjoy his kindness and love every moment of their lives, may be made, according to circumstances — all depending on the development of the children   However, care should always be taken not to present to them, what might be called abstract morals, which the young mind is unable to grasp, and which, if thus forced upon it cannot fail to be injurious to moral development   The aim of all education should be love of the good, beautiful, noble, and sublime, but nothing is more apt to kill this very love ere it is born, than the monotony of dry, dull preaching of morals to young children   Words not so much as deeds—

actual experiences in the life of the child, are its most natural teachers in this important branch of education

FORMS OF BEAUTY
(PLATES XXI AND XXII)

Owing to the larger multiplicity of elementary forms to be made with the triangles, the number of Forms of Beauty is a very large one   Triangle square, right angle, rhomb, hexagon octagon, are all employed, and the great diversity and beauty of the forms produced lend a lasting charm to the child's occupation   Its inventive power and desire, led by law, will find constant satisfaction, and to give satisfaction in the fullest measure should be a prominent feature of all systems of education

FORMS TO BE BUILT WITH FOUR TABLETS

have already been mentioned on page 33 as contained on Plate XXI—D, 48-59   We find more satisfaction by employing

EIGHT TABLETS

In working with them, we can follow th most various principles   Series E 60-69 is formed by doubling the forms produced by four tablets, series F, starting from the fundamental form 70 making one half of the tablets move from left to right the length of one side, with each move   A new series would be produced, if we move from right to left in a similar manner   In these figures sides always touch sides, and corners touch corners—consequently, parts of the same kind

The transition or mediation between these two opposites, the touching of corners and sides would be produced by shortening the movement of the traveling triangle one-half, permitting it to proceed one half side only

But let us return to fundamental form 70   In it, either large sides (hypothenuses) or small sides (catheti) constantly touch one another   The opposite—large side touching small—we have in Fig 82, and by traveling from right to left of half the triangles, series

G, 82 to 87, is produced We would have produced a much larger number of forms, if we had not interrupted progress by turning the triangles produced by Fig 86

In the fundamental forms 70 and 82, the sides touched one another Fig 88 shows that they may touch at the corners only In this figure, the right angles are without, in 89 and 90, they are within Fig 90 is the mediation between 70 and 89, for four tablets touch with their sides (70) four with the corners (89) No 91 is the opposite of 90, full center, (empty center,) and mediation between 88 and 89—(four right angles without, as in 88, and four within, as in 89) It is already seen, from these indications, what a treasure of forms enfolds itself here and how, with

SIXTEEN TABLETS,

it again will be multiplied

It would be impossible to exhaust them Least of all should it be the task of this work to do this, when it is only intended to show how the productive self occupation of the pupil can fittingly be assisted We believe, besides, that we have given a sufficient number of ways on which fantasy may travel, perfectly sure of finding constantly new, beautiful, eye and taste developing formations We, therefore, simply add the series J and K, the first of which is produced by quadrupling some of the elementary forms given at D, 48 to 59, and the second of which indicates how new series of forms of beauty may be developed from each of these forms. It must be evident, even to the casual observer how here also the law of opposites, and their junction, was observed Opposites are 92 and 93 , mediation, 94 and 95 opposites 96 and 97 , mediation, 98, 99, and 100 · opposites, 101 and 102 , mediation, 103, etc

WITH THIRTY-TWO TABLETS

As heretofore, we proceed here also in the same manner, by multiplying the given elements, or by means of further development, according to the law of opposites As an example, we give Series L the members of which are produced by a four-fold junction of the elements 68 and 69 110 and 111 are opposites , 112 and 113 mediative forms

WITH SIXTY FOUR TABLETS

Here, also, the combined activity of many children will result in forms interesting to be looked at, not only by little children There is another feature of this combined activity not to be forgotten The children are busy obeying the same law , the same aim unites them—one helps the other. Thus the conditions of human society—family, community, states, etc ,—are already here shown in their effects A system of education which so to speak, by mere play, leads the child to appreciate those requisites, by compliance with which it can successfully occupy its position as man in the future, certainly deserves the epithet of a natural and rational one.

Figures 114, 115, 116, are enlarged productions from 96 and 97 They are planned in such a way, as to admit of being continued in all directions, and thus serve to carry out the representation of a very large design

After having acted so far, according to indications made here, it is now advisable to start from the fundamental forms presented in the Fifth Gift, and to use them, with the necessary modifications, in farther occupying the pupils with the tablets Fig 117 gives a model, showing how the motives of the Fifth Gift can be used for this purpose

FORMS OF KNOWLEDGE.
(PLATE XXII)

By joining two, four, and eight tablets, we have already become acquainted with the regular figures which may be formed with them, namely, triangle quadrangle (square), right angle, rhomboid, and trapezium (Plate XXII , Figs 118–123)

The tablets are, however, especially qualified to bring to the observation of the child different sizes in equal forms (similar figures) and equal sizes in different forms

Figures 124, 125, and 126 show triangles of which each is the half of the following, and Nos 129, 127 and 128, three squares of that kind Figures 119–123, and 129–131, show the former five, the latter three times the same size in different forms

That the contemplation of these figures, the occupation with them, must tend to facilitate the understanding of geometrical axioms in future, who can doubt? And who can gainsay that mathematical instruction, by means of Froebel's method must needs be facilitated, and better results obtained? That such instruction, then, will be rendered more fruitful for practical life, is a fact which will be obvious to all, who simply glance at our figures, even without a thorough explanation They contain demonstratively the larger number of the axioms in elementary geometry, which relate to the conditions of the plane in regular figures

For the present purpose, it is sufficient if the child learns to distinguish the various kinds of angles, if it knows that the right angles are all equally large, the acute angles smaller, and the obtuse angles larger than a right angle, which the child will easily understand by putting one upon another A deeper insight in the matter must be reserved for the primary department of instruction.

C THE EQUILATERAL TRIANGLE.
(PLATES XXIV AND XXV)

So far the right angle has predominated in the occupations with the tablets, and the acute angle only appeared in subordinate relations. Now it is the latter alone which governs the actions of the child in producing forms and figures

The child will compare the equilateral triangle, which it receives in gifts of 3 6 9, and 12, first with the isosceles right angled tablet already known to him Both have three sides both three angles, but on close observation not only their similarities, but also their dissimilarities will become apparent The three angles of the new triangle are all smaller

than a right angle, are acute angles and the three sides are just alike, hence the name—equilateral—meaning "*equal sided*" triangle

Joining two of these equilateral tablets the child will discover that it cannot form any of the regular figures previously produced No triangle, no square, no right angle, no rhomboid, can be produced, but only a form similar to the latter, a rhomboid with four equal sides To undertake to produce forms of life with these tablets would prove very unsatisfactory Of particular interest however, because presenting entirely new formations, are

THE FORMS OF BEAUTY

The child first receives *three tablets* and will find the various positions of the same towards one another according to the law of opposites and their combination *Vide* Plate XXIV, 1–9

SIX TABLETS

The child will unite his tablets around one common center (Fig 10), form the opposite (Fig 11), and then arrive at the forms of mediation 12, 13, 14, and 15, or it unites three elementary forms each composed of two tablets as done in 16, and forms the opposite 17 and the mediations 18 and 19, or it starts from No 10, turning first 1, then 2, then 3 tablets, outwardly By turning one tablet, 21 and 22, by turning two tablets, 23, 24, 25 26 27 28 and 29 are produced from No 20 This may be continued with 3, 4, and 5 tablets All forms thus received give us elementary forms which may be employed as soon as a larger number of tablets are to be used

NINE TABLETS

As with the right angled triangle, small groups of tablets were combined to form larger figures, so we also do here The elementary forms under A give us in threefold combination the series of forms under C, 30—40, which in course of the occupation may be multiplied at will

TWELVE TABLETS
(PLATE XXV)

Half of the tablets are painted brown, the balance blue. By this difference in color, opposites are rendered more conspicuous, and these twelve tablets thus afford a splendid opportunity for illustrating more forcibly the law of opposites and their combination. Plate XXV shows how, by combination of opposites in the forms a and b, every time the star c is produced. Entirely new series of forms may be produced by employing a larger number of tablets, 18, 24 or 36. We are, however, obliged to leave these representations to the combined inventive powers of teacher and pupil.

FORMS OF KNOWLEDGE

It has been mentioned before, that the previously introduced regular mathematical figures do not appear here as a whole. However, a triangle can be represented by four or nine tablets, a rhomboid by four, six or eight tablets, a trapezium by three, and manifold instructive remarks can be made and experiences gathered in the construction of these figures. But above all, it is the rhombus and hexagon, with which the pupil is to be made acquainted here. The child unites two triangles by joining side to side, and thus produces a rhombus.

The child compares the sides—are they alike? What is their direction? Are they parallel? Two and two have the same direction, and are therefore parallel.

The child now examines the angles and finds that two and two are of equal size. They are not right angles. Triangles, smaller than right angles, he knows, are called acute angles, and he hears now that the larger ones are called obtuse angles. The teacher may remark that the latter are twice the size of the former ones. By these remarks the pupil will gradually receive a correct idea of the rhombus and of the qualities by which it is distinguished from the quadrangle, right angle, trapezium and rhomboid.

In the same manner, the hexagon gives occasion for interesting and instructive questions and answers. How many sides has it? How many are parallel? How many angles does it contain? What kind of angles are they? How large are they as compared with the angles of the equal sided triangle? Twice as large.

The power of observation and the reasoning faculties are constantly developed by such conversation, and the results of such exercises are of more importance than all the knowledge that may be acquired in the meantime.

The greater part of this occupation, however, is not within the Kinder Garten proper, but belongs to the realm of the Primary School Department. If they are introduced in the former, they are intended only to swell the sum of general experience in regard to the qualities of things, whereas in the latter, they serve as a foundation for real knowledge in the department of mathematics.

D. THE OBTUSE-ANGLED TRIANGLE WITH TWO SIDES ALIKE.
(PLATES XXVI AND XXVII)

The child receives a box with sixty-four obtuse angled tablets. It examines one of them and compares it with the right-angled triangle, with two sides alike. It has two sides alike, has also two acute angles, but the third angle is larger than the right angle; it is an obtuse angle, and the tablet is, therefore, an obtuse-angled triangle with two sides alike.

The pupil then unites two and two tablets by joining their sides, corners, sides and corners, and vice versa, as shown in Figs 1–8, on Plate XXVI.

The next preliminary exercise, is the combination, by fours, of elementary forms thus produced. Peculiarly beautiful, mosaic-like forms of beauty result from this process. The Figs 9–15 afford examples which were produced by combination of two opposites, a and b, or by mediative forms c and d. In

Figs 16–22 we have finally some few samples of forms of life.

The forms of knowledge which may be produced, afford opportunity to repeat what has been taught and learned previously about proportion of form and size   In the Primary School the geometrical proportions are further introduced, by which means the knowledge of the pupils, in regard to angles, as to the position they occupy in the triangle, can be successfully developed by practical observation, without the necessity of ever dealing in mere abstractions

E   THE RIGHT-ANGLED TRIANGLE WITH NO EQUAL SIDES

(PLATES XXVIII AND XXIX)

The little box with fifty-six tablets of the above description, each of which is half the size of the obtuse-angled triangle, enables the child to represent a goodly number of forms of life, as shown on Plate XXIX

In producing them, sufficient opportunities will present themselves, to let the child find out the qualities of the new occupation material

A comparison with the right angled triangle with two equal sides will facilitate the matter greatly

On the whole, however. the process of development may be pursued, as repeatedly indicated on previous occasions

The variety of the forms of beauty to be laid with these tablets, is especially founded on their combination in twos   Plate XXVIII, Figs 1–6, shows the forms produced by join ing equal sides

In similar manner, the child has to find out the forms which will be the result of joining unlike sides, like corners, unlike corners, and finally, corners and sides

By a fourfold combination of such element ary forms the child receives the material, (Figs 7–18,) to produce a large number of forms of beauty similar to those given under 19–22

For the purpose, also of presenting to the child s observation, in a new shape, proportions of form and size, in the production of forms of knowledge, these tablets are very serviceable.

Like the previous tablets, these also, and a following set of similar tablets, are used in the Primary Department for enlivening the instruction in Geometry   It is believed that nothing has ever been invented to so facilitate, and render interesting to teacher and pupil the instruction in this so important branch of education as the tablets forming the Seventh Gift of Froebel's Occupation Material, the use of which is commenced with the children when they have entered the second year of their Kinder Garten discipline.

THE EIGHTH GIFT.

————•••————

STAFFS FOR LAYING OF FIGURES

(PLATES XXX TO XXXIII)

As the *tablets* of the Seventh Gift are nothing but an embodiment of the *planes* surrounding or limiting the *cube*, and as these *planes*, limits of the cube, are nothing but the *representations* of the extension in *length*, *breadth, and height*, already contained in the sphere and ball, so also the staffs are derived from the cube, forming as they do, and here bodily representing its *edges* But they are also contained in the tablets, because the plane is thought of, as consisting of a continued or repeated line, and this may be illustrated by placing a sufficient number of one inch long staffs side by side, and close together, until a square is formed

The staffs lead us another step farther, from the material, bodily, toward the realm of abstractions

By means of the tablets, we were enabled to produce flat images of bodies, the slats, which, as previously mentioned, form a transition from plane to line, gave, it is true, the outlines of forms, but these outlines still retained a certain degree of the plane about them, in the staffs, however, we obtain the material to draw the outlines of objects, by bodily lines, as perfectly as it can possibly be done

The laying of staffs is a favorite occupation with all children Their fantasy sees in them the most different objects,—stick, yard measure, candle, in short, they are to them representatives of every thing straight

Our staffs are of the thickness of a line (one twelfth of an inch), and are cut in vari

ous lengths The child, holding the staff in hand, is asked What do you hold in your hand? How do you hold it? Perpendicularly Can you hold it in any other way? Yes! I can hold it horizontally Still in another way? Slanting from left above, to right below, or from right above to left below

Lay your staff upon the table How does it lie? In what other direction can you place it? (Plate XXX A)

The child receives a *second staff* How many staffs have you now? Now try to form something The child lays a standing cross (Fig 4) You certainly can lay many other and more beautiful things, but let us see what else we may produce of this cross, by moving the horizontal staff, by half its length, (Fig B 4 to 14) Starting from a lying cross (C. 15—23) or from a pair of open tongs, (where two acute and two obtuse angles are formed by the crossing staffs,) and proceeding similarly as with B, we will produce all positions which two staffs can occupy, relative to one another, except the parallel, and this will give ample opportunity to refresh, and more deeply impress upon the pupil's mind, all that has been introduced so far, concerning perpendicular, horizontal, and oblique lines, and of right, acute and obtuse angles With two staffs, we can also form little figures, which show some slight resemblance with things around us By them we enliven the power of recollection and imagination of the child, exercise his ability of comparison, increase his

treasure of ideas, and develop, in all these
his power of perception and conception—the
most indispensable requisites for disciplining
the mind

Our plates give representations of the following objects .

WITH TWO STAFFS

Fig 24 A Playing Table.
Fig 25 A Weather-vane
Fig 26 A Pickax
Fig 27 An Angle measure (Carpenter's square.)
Fig 28 A Candle stick
Fig 29 Two Candles
Fig 30 Rails.
Fig 31 Roof

WITH THREE STAFFS

Fig 32 A Kitchen Table
Fig 33 A Garden Rake
Fig 34 A Flail
Fig 35 An Umbrella
Fig 36 A Hay Fork
Fig 37 A Small Flag.
Fig 38 A Steamer
Fig 39 A Whorl
Fig 40 A Star

WITH FOUR STAFFS

Fig. 41 A Small Looking glass
Fig 42 A Wooden Chair
Fig 43 A Wash-bench
Fig 44 Kitchen Table with Candle
Fig 45 A Crib
Fig. 46 A Kennel
Fig 47 Sugar loaf
Fig 48 Flower pot
Fig 49 Signal-post
Fig 50 Flower-stand
Fig 51 Crucifix
Fig 52 A Grate

WITH FIVE STAFFS

Fig 53 Signal Flag of R R Guard.
Fig 54 Chest of Drawers
Fig 55. A Cottage

Fig 56 A Steeple
Fig 57 A Funnel
Fig 58 A Beer Bottle
Fig 59 A Bath Tub
Fig 60 A (broken) Plate
Fig 61 A Roof
Fig 62 A Hat
Fig 63 A Chair
Fig 64 A Lamp Shade
Fig 65 A Wine glass.
Fig 66 A Grate

WITH SIX STAFFS.

Fig 67 A Large Frame
Fig 68 A Flag
Fig 69 A Barn
Fig 70 A Boat
Fig 71 A Reel
Fig 72 A Small Tree.
Fig 73. A Round Table.

WITH SEVEN STAFFS

Fig 74 A Window.
Fig 75 A Stretcher
Fig 76 A Dwelling-house
Fig 77 Steeple with Lightning rod.
Fig 78 A Balance
Fig. 79 Piano forte
Fig 80 A Bridge with Three Spans.
Fig 81 An Inn Sign
Fig 82 Crucifix and Two Candles.
Fig 83 Tombstone and Cross.
Fig 84 Rail Fence
Fig 85 Garret Window.
Fig 86 Flower Spade
Fig 87 A Star Flower

WITH EIGHT STAFFS

Fig 88 Book-shelves
Fig 89. Church, with Steeple.
Fig 90 Tombstone and Cross
Fig 91. Gas Lantern
Fig 92 Windmill
Fig 93 A Tower
Fig 94 An Umbrella
Fig 95 A Carrot
Fig 96 A Flower pot.

These exercises are to be continued with a larger number of staffs The hints given above, will enable the teacher to conduct the laying of staffs in a manner interesting, as well as useful, for her pupils

It is advisable to guide the activity of the child occasionally in another direction The pupils may all be called upon to lay tables, which can be produced from two to ten staffs, or houses which can be laid with eighteen staffs

Another change in this occupation can be introduced by employing two, four, or eight times, divided staffs It is obvious that, in this manner, the figures may often assume a greater similarity and better proportions than is possible if only staffs of the same length are employed

If a staff is not entirely broken through, but only bent with a break on one side, an angle is produced If a staff forms several such angles it can be used to represent a curved or rounded line, and by so doing a new feature is introduced to the class

Staffs are also employed for representing forms of beauty. The previous, or simultaneous occupation with the building blocks, and tablets, will assist the child in producing the same in great variety Figures 121—124 on Plate XXXIII belong to this class of representations

Combination of the occupation material of several, or all children taking part in the exercises, will lead to the production of larger forms of life, or beauty, which in the Primary Department, can even be extended to representing whole landscapes, in which the material is augmented by the introduction of saw dust to represent foliage, grass, land, moss, etc Plate XXXIII gives, under Fig 120, a specimen of such a production—on a very reduced scale

By means of combination, the children often produce forms which afford them great pleasure, and repay them for the careful perseverance and skill employed They often express the wish that they might be able to show the production to father, or mother, or sister, or friend But this they cannot do, as the staffs will separate when taken up

We should assist the little ones in carrying out their desire of giving pleasure to others by showing to, or presenting them with the result of their own industry, in portable form

By wetting the ends of the staffs with mucilage, or binding them together with needle and thread, or placing them on substantial paper, we can grant their desire, and make them happy, and be sure of their thanks for our efforts

We employ the same means of rendering permanent the production of staff laying in our instruction in reading, where letters are fastened to paper by mucilage, thus impressing upon the child's mind more lastingly, the visible signs of the sounds he has learned

But we have still another means of rendering these representations permanent, and it is by *drawing*, which, on its own account, is to be practiced in the most elementary manner We begin the drawing, as will hereafter be shown, as a special branch of occupation, as soon as the child has reached its third or fourth year

The child is provided with a slate, upon whose surface, a net work of horizontal and perpendicular lines is drawn Instead of laying the staff upon the table, the child places it upon the slate Taking the staff from its place, he draws with the slate pencil, in its stead, a line as long as the staff, in the same direction He draws the perpendicular staff The horizontal, slantingly laid staff, is drawn in all its variations in like manner, perpendicular, and horizontal, perpendicular and oblique, or horizontal and oblique staffs are brought in contact with one another, and these connections reproduced by drawing

The method of laying staffs is in general the same, applied for drawing, the latter, however, progresses less rapidly It is advisable to combine staffs in regular figures, triangles and squares, and to find out in a small number of such figures all possible combinations according to the law of opposites Plates XXIV and XXV will furnish material for this purpose

All these occupations depend on the larger or smaller number of staffs employed, they therefore afford means for increasing and strengthening the knowledge of the child

The pupil, however, is much more decidedly introduced into the elements of ciphering, when the staffs are placed into his hands for this specific purpose We do not hesitate to make the assertion that there is no material better fitted to teach the rudiments in figures, as also the more advanced steps in arithmetic, than Froebel's staffs, and that by their introduction, all other material is rendered useless A few packages of the staffs in the hands of the pupil is all that is needed in the Kinder Garten proper, and the following Department of the Primary

The children receive a package with ten staffs each Take one staff and lay it perpendicularly on the table Lay another at the side of it How many staffs are now before you? Twice one makes two

Lay still another staff upon the table How many are there now? One and one and one—two and one are three

Still another, etc, etc until all ten staffs are placed in a similar manner upon the table Now take away one staff How many remain? Ten less one leaves nine Take away another staff from these nine How many are left? Nine less one leaves eight Take another, this leaves——? seven, etc, etc, until all the staffs are taken one by one from the table, and are in the child's hand again Take two staffs and lay them upon the table, and place two others at some distance from them (|| ||) How many are now on the table? Two and two are *four* Lay two more staffs beside these four staffs How many are there now? Four and two are *six* Two more How many are there now? Six and two are *eight* And still another two How many now? Eight and two are *ten*

The child has learned to add staffs by twos If we do the opposite, he will also learn to subtract by twos In similar manner we proceed with *three, four,* and *five* After that, we *alternate*, with addition and subtraction For instance, we lay three times two staffs upon the table and take away twice two, adding again four times two Finally we give up the

equality of the number and alternate, by ad
ding different numbers We lay upon the
table 2 and 3 staffs=5, adding 2=7 adding
3=10 This affords opportunity to intro
duce 6 and 9, as a whole, more frequently
than was the case in previous exercises, In
subtraction we observe the same method, and
introduce exercises in which subtraction and
addition alternate with unequal numbers
Lay 6 staffs upon the table, take 2 away, add
4, take away 1, add 3, and ask the child how
many staffs are on the table, after each of
these operations

In like manner, as the child learned the
figures from one to ten, and added and sub
tracted with them as far as the number of 10
staffs admitted, it will now learn to use the
10's up to 100 Packages of 10 staffs are
distributed It treats each package as it did
before the single staff One is laid upon the
table, and the child says, 'Once ten,'' add a
second, "Twice ten," a third, "Three times
ten," etc Subsequently it is told, that it is
not customary to say twice, or two times ten,
but twenty, not three times ten, but thirty,
etc This experience will take root so much
the sooner, in his memory, and become
knowledge, as all this is the result of his own
activity

As soon as the child has acquired sufficient
ability in adding and subtracting by tens, the
combination of units and tens is introduced

The pupil receives two packages of ten
staffs—places one of them upon the table,
opens the second and adds its staffs one by
one to the ten contained in the whole pack
age He learns 10 and 1=11, 10 and 2=12,
10 and 3=13, until 10 and 10=20 staffs
Gathering the 10 loose staffs the child re
ceives another package and places it beside
the first whole package 10 and 10=20
staffs Then he adds one of the loose staffs,
and says 20 and 1=21, 20 and 2=22, etc.
Another package of 10 brings the number to
31, etc, etc, up to 91 staffs In this manner
he learns 22 32, up to 92, 23 to 93, and 100
and to add and subtract within this limit

To be taught addition and subtraction in
this manner, is to acquire sound knowledge,
founded on self-activity and experience, and
is far superior to any kind of mind killing
memorizing usually employed in this connec
tion

If addition and subtraction are each other's
opposites, so addition and multiplication on
the one hand and subtraction and division
on the other, are oppositionally equal, or,
rather, multiplication and division are short-
ened addition and subtraction

In addition, when using equal numbers of
staffs, the child finds that by adding 2 and 2
and 2 and 2 staffs it receives 8 staffs and is
told that this may also be expressed by saying
4 times 2 staffs are 8 staffs It will be easy
to see how to proceed with division, after the
hints given above

It has been previously mentioned that for
the representation of forms of life and beauty
the staffs frequently need to be broken This
provides material for teaching fractions in the
meantime The child learns by observation
$\frac{1}{2}$ staff, $\frac{1}{3}$ $\frac{1}{4}$, $\frac{1}{5}$, etc The proportion of the
part or of several equal parts to the whole,
becomes clear to him, and finally it learns to
add and subtract equal fractions, in elementary form, in the same rational manner

Let none of our readers misunderstand us
as intimating that all this should be accomplished in the Kinder Garten proper

Enough has been accomplished if the child
in the Kinder Garten, by means of staffs and
other material of occupation, has been en
abled to have a clear understanding of figures
in general

This will be the basis for further development in addition, subtraction multiplication
and division in the Primary Department

It now remains to add the necessary advice
in regard to the introduction and representation with staffs of the *numerals* In order to
make the children understand what *numerals*
are, use the blackboard and show them that
if we wish to mark down how many *staffs*,
blocks, or other things each of the children

have, we might make one line for each staff, block, etc   Write then *one* small perpendicular line on the blackboard, saying in writing, Charles has *one staff*, making *two* lines *below* the first, continue by saying, Emma has *two blocks*, again, making *three lines*, Ernest has *three rubber balls*, and so on until you have written ten lines, always giving the name of the child and stating how many objects it has Then write opposite each row of lines to the right, the *Arabic* figure expressing the number of lines, and remark that instead of using so many lines, we can also use these figures, which we call *numerals* Then represent with the little staff these Arabic figures, some of which require the bending of some of the staffs, on account of the curved lines

After the children have learned that the figures which we use for marking down the *number of things* are called numerals, exercises of the following character may be introduced

How many hands has each of you? Two The numeral 2 is written on the board How many fingers on each hand? Five This is written also on the board—5 How many walls has this room? Four Write this figure also on the board How many days in the week are the children in the Kinder Garten? Six days The 6 is also written on the board

Then repeat, and let the children repeat after you, as an exercise in speaking, and at the same time, for the purpose of recollecting the numerals

Each child has 2 hands, on each hand are 5 fingers, this room has 4 walls,—always emphasizing the numerals, and pointing to them when they are named

The children may then count the objects in the room, or elsewhere, and then lay, with their staffs, the numerals expressing the number they have found, speaking in the mean time, a sentence asserting the fact which they have stated

After having introduced the numerals in this manner, the teacher, on some following day, may proceed to reading exercises

The second part of this Guide contains systematically arranged material for instruction in reading, according to the phonetic method

Suffice it to say, that it is begun in the same manner in which numerals were introduced As by means of numerals, I could mark on the blackboard the number of things, so I can also mark on the board the *names of things*, their *qualities* and *actions* In doing this I write *words*, and *words* consist of *letters* Besides the words expressing names of things, their *qualities* and *actions*, which are the most important words in every language there are other words which are used for other purposes Such words are, for example, no, now, never Should I ask you, is any one of you asleep, what would you answer? "No, sir We are all awake" I will write the little word "*no*," on the blackboard, because it is the most important word in your answer There it stands, "*no*" And now I will ask you "Have you ever been in a Kinder Garten?" "Yes, sir, we are now in a Kinder Garten school" I will write on the board the little word, "*now*" There it stands, "*now*," and another question I will now ask you "Should we ever kill an animal for the mere pleasure of hurting it?" "No, sir, *never*" I will also write the word "*never*," on the board There it is, "*never*" I will now pronounce these three words for you, and each of you will repeat them in the same manner in which I do N——o! N——ow! N——ever! Children, in repeating, always dwell on the *n* sound longer than on any other part of the word They are then *led* to observe the similarity of sound in pronouncing the three words, then to observe the similarity of the first letter in all of them, and finally the dissimilarity of the remaining part of the words in sound, and its representations—the letters

I will now take away these words from the blackboard, and write something else upon it. I again write the "*n*," and the children will soon recognize it as the letter previously shown

For the continuation of instruction in reading, we refer the reader to the second part of the Guide," where all necessary information on this important branch of instruction will be found

As the occupation with laying staffs, is one

of the earliest in the Kinder Garten, and is employed in teaching numerals, and reading and writing, and drawing also, it is evident how important a material of occupation was supplied by Froebel, in introducing the staffs as one of his Kinder-Garten Gifts

THE NINTH GIFT.

WHOLE AND HALF RINGS FOR LAYING FIGURES

(PLATE XXXIV)

IMMEDIATELY connected with the staffs, or straight lines, Froebel gives the representatives of the rounded, curved lines in a box containing twenty four whole and forty eight half circles of two different sizes made of wire We have heretofore introduced the curved line by bending the staff, this, however, was a rather imperfect representation The rings now introduced supply the means of representing a curved line perfectly, besides enabling us by their different sizes to show ' the one within another " more plainly than it could be done with the staffs, as the *above upon below, aside of each other*, etc, could well be represented, but not the "*within*" in a perfectly clear manner

This Gift is introduced in the same way as all other previous Gifts were introduced, and the rules by which this occupation is carried on must be clear to every one who has followed us in our 'Guide" to this point

The child receives one whole ring and two half rings of the larger size Looking at the whole ring the children observe that there is neither beginning nor end in the ring—that it represents the circle, in which there is neither beginning nor end. With the half ring, they have two ends, half rings, like half circles and all other parts of the circle or curved lines, have two ends Two of the half rings

form one whole ring or circle, and the children are asked to show this by experiment, (Fig 1, Plate XXXIV) Various observations can be made by the children, accompanied by remarks on the part of the teacher Whenever the child combined two cubes, two tablets staffs or slats with one another, in all cases where corners and angles and ends were concerned in this combination, corners and angles were again produced The two half rings or half circles, however, do not form any angles Neither could closed space be produced by two bodies, planes, nor lines —the two half circles, however, close tightly up to each other, so that no opening remains

The child now places the two half circles in opposite directions, (Fig 2) Before the ends touched one another, now the middle of the half circles, previously a closed space was formed, now both half circles are open, and where they touch one another, angles appear

Mediation is formed in Fig 3, where both half circles touch each other at one end and remain open, or, as indicated by the dotted line, join at end and middle, thereby enclosing a small plane and forming angles in the meantime

Two more half circles are presented The child forms Fig 4, and develops by moving the half circles in the direction from without, to within Fig 5, 6, 7, and 8

The number of circles is increased Fig 9, 10, and 11 show some forms built of 8 half circles

All these forms are, owing to the nature of the circular line, forms of *beauty* or beautiful forms of life, and, therefore, the occupation with these rings, is of such importance The child produces forms of beauty with other material, it is true, but the curved line suggests to him in a higher degree than anything else, ideas of the beautiful, and the simplest combinations of a small number of half and whole circles, also bear in themselves the stamps of beauty

If the fact cannot be refuted that merely looking at the beautiful, favorably impresses the mind of the grown person, in regard to direction of its development, enabling him to more fully appreciate the good and true, and noble, and sublime, this influence upon the tender and pliable soul of the child, must needs be greater, and more lasting Without believing in the doctrine of two inimical natures in man, said to be in constant conflict with each other, we do believe that the

talents and disposition in human nature are subject to the possibility of being developed in two opposite directions It is this possibility, which conditions the necessity of education, the necessity of employing every means to give the dormant inclinations and tastes in the child. a direction toward the true, and good, and beautiful,—in one word, toward the ideal Among these means, stands pre-eminently a rational and timely development of the sense of beauty, upon which Froebel lays so much stress

Showing the young child objects of art which are far beyond the sphere of its appreciation, however, will assist this development, much less than to carefully guard that its surroundings contain, and show the fundamental requisites of beauty, viz order, cleanliness, simplicity. and harmony of form, and giving assistance to the child in the active representation to the beautiful in a manner adapted to the state of development in the child himself

Like forms laid with staffs, those represented with rings and half rings also, are imitated by the children by drawing them on slate or paper

THE TENTH GIFT.

THE MATERIAL FOR DRAWING

(PLATES XXXV TO XLVI)

ONE of the earliest occupations of the child should be methodical drawing Froebel s opinion and conviction on this subject, deviates from those of other educators, as much as in other respects Froebel, however, does not advocate drawing as it is usually practiced, which on the whole, is nothing else but a more or less thoughtless mechanical copy

ing The method advanced by Froebel, is invented by him, and perfected in accordance with his general educational principles

The pedagogical effect of the customary method of instruction in drawing rests in many cases simply in the amount of trouble caused the pupil in surmounting technical difficulties Just for that reason it should be abandoned entirely for the youngest pupils, for the difficulties in many cases are too great for the child to cope with It is a work of Sisyphus, *labor without result*, naturally tending to extirpate the pleasure of the child in its occupation, and the unavoidable consequence is that the majority of people will never reach the point where they can enjoy the fruits of their endeavors

If we acknowledge that Froebel's educational principles are correct, namely, that all manifestations of the child's life are manifestations of an innate instinctive desire for development, and therefore should be fostered and developed by a rational education, in accordance with the laws of nature Drawing should be commenced with the third year, nay, its preparatory principles should be introduced at a still earlier period

With all the gifts, hitherto introduced, the children were able to study and represent forms and figures Thus they have been occupied, as it were, in *drawing with bodies* This developed their fantasy, and taste, giving them in the meantime correct ideas of the solid, plane, and the embodied line

A desire soon awakes in the child, to represent by *drawing* these lines and planes, these forms and objects He is desirous of representation when he requests the mother to tell him a story, explain a picture He is occupied in representation when breathing against the window pane, and scrawling on it with its finger, or when trying to make figures in the sand with a little stick Each child is delighted to show what it can make and should be assisted in every way to regulate this desire

Drawing not only develops the power of representing things the mind has perceived, but affords the best means for testing how far they have been perceived correctly

It was Froebel's task to invent a method adapted to the tender age of the child, and its slight dexterity of hand, and in the mean time to satisfy the claim of all his occupations. i e, that the child should not simply imitate, but proceed, self-actingly, to perform work which enables him to reflect, reason, and finally to invent himself

Both claims have been most ingeniously satisfied by Froebel He gives the three years' old child a slate, one side of which is covered by a net work of engraved lines (one-fourth of an inch apart), and he gives him in addition, thereto, the law of opposites and their mediation as a rule for h s activity.

The lines of the net work guide the child in moving the pencil, they assist it in measuring and comparing situation and position, size and relative center, and sides of objects This facilitates the work greatly, and in consequence of this important assistance the childs' desire for work is materially increased, whereas, obstacles in the earliest attempts at all kinds of work must necessarily discourage the beginner

Drawing on the slate, with slate pencil is followed by drawing on paper with lead pencil The paper of the drawing books is ruled like the slates It is advisable to begin and continue the exercises in drawing on paper, in like manner as those on the slate were begun and continued, with this difference only, that owing to the progress made and skill obtained by the child, less repetitions may be needed to bring the pupil to perfection here, as was necessary in the use of the slate

It has been repeatedly suggested, that whenever a new material for occupation is introduced, the teacher should comment upon, or enter into conversation with the children, about the same, the difference between drawing on the slate and on paper, and the material used for both may give rise to many remarks and instructive conversation

It may be mentioned that the slate is first used, because the children can easily correct mistakes by wiping out what they have made, and that they should be much more careful in drawing on paper, as their productions can not appear perfectly clean and neat if it should be necessary to use the rubber often

Slate and slate pencil are of the same material, paper and lead pencil are two very different things   On the slate the lines and figures
drawn, appear white on darker ground   On
the paper, lines and figures appear black on
white ground

More advanced pupils use colored lead
pencils instead of the common black lead
pencils   This adds greatly to the appearance of the figures, and also enables the child
to combine colors tastefully and fittingly   For
the development of their sense of color, and
of taste, these colored mosaic like figures are
excellent practice

Drawing, as such, requires observation, attention, conception of the whole and its parts
the recollection of all, power of invention and
combination of thought   Thus, by it, mind
and fantasy are enriched with clear ideas and
true and beautiful pictures   For a free and
active development of the senses, especially
eye and feeling, drawing can be made of in-
calculable benefit to the child, when its natural instinct for it is correctly guided at its
very awakening

Our Plates XXXV to XLVI show the systematic course pursued in the drawing department of the Kinder Garten   The child is first
occupied by

THE PERPENDICULAR LINE
(PLATES XXXV TO XXXVIII)

The teacher draws on the slate a perpen-
dicular line of a single length ($\frac{1}{4}$ of an inch),
saying while so doing I draw a line of a single
length downward   She then (leaving the line
on the slate, or wiping it out) requires the
child to do the same.   She should show that
the line she made commenced exactly at the
crossing point of two lines of the network,
and also ended at such a point

Care should be exercised that the child
hold the pencil properly, not press too much
or too little on the slate, that the lines drawn
be as equally heavy as possible, and that each
single line be produced by one single stroke
of the pencil   The teacher should occasion-

ally ask. What are you doing? or, what have
you done? and the child should always an
swer in a complete sentence, showing that it
works understandingly   Soon the lines may
be drawn upwards also, and then they may
be made alternately up and down over the
entire slate, until the child has acquired a certain degree of ability in handling the pencil.

The child is then required to draw a per
pendicular line of two lengths, and advances
slowly to lines of three, four and five lengths,
(Plate XXXV, Figs 2—5)

With the number five Froebel stops on
this step   One to five are sufficiently known,
even to the child three years old, by the
number of his fingers.

The productions thus far accomplished are
now combined   The child draws, side by
side of one another, lines of one and two
lengths (Fig 6), of one, two and three lengths
(Fig 7), of one, two, three and four lengths
(Fig 8), and finally lines of one, two, three,
four and five lengths (Fig 9)   It always forms
by so doing a right-angled triangle   We
have noticed already, in using the tablets, that
right angled triangles can lie in many different
ways   The triangle (Fig 9 and 10) can also
assume various positions   In Fig 10 the
five lines stand on the base line—the smallest
is the first, the largest the last, the right angle is to the right below   In Fig 11 the opposite is found—the five lines hang on the
base-line, the largest comes first, the smallest
last, and the right angle is to the left above
Figs 12 and 13 are forms of mediation of 10
and 11.

The child should be induced to find Figs
11 to 13 himself   Leading him to understand
the points of Fig 10 exactly, he will have no
difficulty in representing the opposite   Instead
of drawing the smallest line first, he will draw
the longest, instead of drawing it downward,
he will move his pencil upward, or at least
begin to draw on the line which is bounded
above, and thus reach 11   By continued reflection, entirely within the limits of his capa-
bilities, he will succeed in producing 12 and 13

Thus by a different way of combination of five perpendicular lines, four forms have been produced, consisting of equal parts, being, however, unlike, and therefore oppositionally alike

Each of these figures is a whole in itself But as every thing is always part of a larger whole, so also these figures serve as elements for more extensive formations

In this feature of Froebel's drawing method, in which we progress from the simple to the more complicated in the most natural and logical manner, unite parts to a whole and recognize the former as members of the latter, discover the like in opposites, and the mediation of the latter, unquestionable guarantee is given that the delight of the child will be renewed and increased, throughout the whole course of instruction Let Figs 10—13 be so united that the right angles connect in the center (Fig 14), and again unite them so that all right angles are on the outside (Fig 15) Figs 14 and 15 are opposites No 14 is a square with filled inside and standing on one corner, No 15 one resting on its base, with hollow middle In 14 the right angles are just in the middle, in 15 they are the most outward corners In the forms of mediation (16 and 17), they are, it is true, on the middle line, but in the meantime on the out lines of the figures formed In the other forms of mediation, (Figs 18, 19, etc) they lie altogether on the middle line, but two in the middle, and two in the limits of the figure.

Thus we have again, in Figs 18—22 four forms consisting of exactly the same parts, which therefore are equal and still have qualities of opposites In the meantime, they are fit to be used as simple elements of following formations In Fig 22 they are combined into a star with filled middle, in Fig 23, it is shown how a star with hollow middle may be formed of them (The Fig 23, on Plate XXXVI, does not show the lower part, on Plate XXII, Fig 97, Gift Seventh, the whole star is shown) Here, too, numerous

forms of mediation may be produced, but we will work at present with our simple elements

Owing to the similarity in the method of drawing to that employed in the laying of the right angled, isosceles triangle, it is natural that we should here also arrive at the so called rotation figures, by grouping our triangles with their acute angles toward the middle (Figs 24 and 25) or arrange them around a hollow square (Figs 26 and 27)

Figs 28 and 29 are forms of mediation between 24 and 25, and at the same time between 14 and 15

All these forms again serve as material for new inventions As an example, we produce Fig 30, composed of Figs 28 and 29

The number of positions in which our original elements (Figs 10—13) can be placed by one another, is herewith not exhausted by far, as the initiated will observe Simple and easy as this method is rendered by natural laws, it is hardly necessary to refer to the tablets (Plates XXI to XXIX) which will suggest a sufficient number of new motives for further combinations

As previously remarked, the slate is exchanged for a drawing book as soon as the progress of the child warrants this change It affords a peculiar charm to the pupil to see his productions assume a certain durability and permanency enabling him to measure, by them, the progress of growing strength and ability

So far the triangles produced by co arrangement of our five lines, were right-angled Other triangles, however, can be produced also This, however, requires more practice and security in handling the pencil

Figs 31 and 32 show an arrangement of the 5 lines, of acute angled (equilateral) triangles, Figs 31 and 32 being opposites Their union gives the opposites 33 and 34, finally the combination of these two, Fig 35

In the last three figures we also meet now the obtuse angle This finds its separate representation in the manner introduced in Fig 36, opposition according to position is given in Fig 37, mediation in Figs 38 and

39, and the combination of these four elements in one rhomboid in Fig 40 The four obtuse angles are turned inwardly Fig 42, the opposite of 40, is produced by arranging the triangles in such a manner that the obtuse angles are turned outwardly Fig 41 presents the form of mediation Another one might be produced by arranging the 4 obtuse angled triangles represented in Nos 36, 37, 38, and 39 in such a manner as to have 39 left above, 37 right above, 36 left below, and

38 right below Thus $\dfrac{39}{36}\Big|\dfrac{37}{38}$

It is evident that with obtuse angled triangles as with right angled triangles, combinations can be produced Indeed, the pupil who has grown into the systematic plan of development and combination will soon be enabled to unite given elements in manifold ways , he will produce stars with filled and hollow middle, rotation forms, etc , and his mental and physical power and capacity will be developed and strengthened greatly by such inventive exercise.

Side by side with invention of forms of beauty and knowledge, the representation of forms of life, take place, in free individual activity The child forms, of lines of one length, a plate, (Fig 43) or a star, (Fig 44,) of lines of one and two lengths a cross, (Fig 45) of lines up to 4 lengths, it represents a coffee-mill, (Fig 46,) and employs the whole material of perpendicular lines at his command in the construction of a large building with part of a wall connected with it (Fig 47) Equal consideration, however, is to be bestowed upon the opposite of the perpendicular,

THE HORIZONTAL LINE

(PLATE XXXIX)

The child learns to draw lines of a single length below each other, then lines of 2, 3, 4, and 5 lengths, (Figs 1—5) It arranges them also beside each other, (Figs 6—8) unites lines of 1 and 2 lengths, (Fig 9,) of 1, 2, and 3 lengths, (Fig 10,) of 1 to 4 lengths, (Fig 11) finally of 1 to 5 lengths, thereby producing

the right angled triangle 12, its opposite 13, and forms of mediation 14 and 15 The pupil arranges the elements into a square with filled middle, (Fig 16) with hollow middle, (Fig 17) produces the forms of mediation,

(Fig 18, $\dfrac{c}{b}\Big|\dfrac{a}{d}$ and $\dfrac{d}{a}\Big|\dfrac{b}{c}$) and continues to treat the horizontal line just as it has been taught to do with the perpendicular (By turning the Plates XXXV to XXXVIII , the figures on them will serve as figures with horizontal lines) Rotation forms, larger figures, acute and obtuse angled triangles can be formed , forms of beauty, knowledge and life are also invented here, (Fig 19, adjustable lamp , Fig 20, key , Fig 21 pigeon house ,) and after the child has accomplished all this, it arrives finally, in a most natural way, at the

COMBINATION OF PERPENDICULAR AND HORIZONTAL LINES

(PLATES XL TO XLII)

First, lines of one single length are combined , we already have four forms different as to position, (Fig 1) Then follow the combination of 2, 3, 4, 5—fold lengths, (Figs 2—5) with each of which 4 opposites as to position are possible As previously, lines of 1 to 5—fold lengths are united to triangles, so now the angles are united and Fig 6 is produced Its opposite, 7 and the forms of mediation, can be easily found A union of these four elements appears in the square, Fig 8 , opposite Fig 9 In Fig 8, the right angles are turned toward the middle, and the middle is full In Fig 9, the reverse is the case Forms of mediation easily found We have in Figs

8 and 9 the combinations $\dfrac{a}{d}\Big|\dfrac{c}{b}$ and $\dfrac{b}{c}\Big|\dfrac{d}{a}$

Let the following be constructed $\dfrac{d}{a}\Big|\dfrac{b}{c}$,

$\dfrac{c}{b}\Big|\dfrac{a}{d}$, $\dfrac{c}{d}\Big|\dfrac{a}{b}$, $\dfrac{a}{d}\Big|\dfrac{c}{b}$, $\dfrac{a}{d}\Big|\dfrac{b}{c}$, $\dfrac{d}{a}\Big|\dfrac{c}{b}$, $\dfrac{c}{b}\Big|\dfrac{d}{a}$, $\dfrac{a}{c}\Big|\dfrac{c}{d}$.

$\dfrac{b}{d}\Big|\dfrac{c}{a}$, $\dfrac{a}{c}\Big|\dfrac{d}{b}$

If perpendicular and horizontal lines can be united only to form right angles, we have previously seen that perpendicular as well as horizontal lines may be combined to obtuse and acute angled triangles The same is possible, if they are united Fig 10 gives us an example All perpendicular lines are so arranged as to form obtuse angled triangles By their combination with the horizontal lines, the element 10^a is produced, its opposite 10^b, and the forms of mediation 10^c and 10^d whose combination forms Fig 10

As in Fig 10, the perpendicular lines form an obtuse angled triangle, so the horizontal lines, and finally both kinds of lines can at the same time be arranged into obtuse angled triangles

Thus a series of new elements is produced, whose systematic employment the teacher should take care to facilitate (The scheme given in the above may be used for this purpose)

So far we have only formed angles of lines equal in length ; but lines of unequal lengths may be combined for this purpose Exactly in the same manner as lines of a single length were treated, the child now combines the line of a single length with that of two lengths, then, in the same way, the line of two lengths with that of four lengths, that of three with that of six, that of four with that of eight, and finally the line of five lengths with that of ten The combination of these angles affords new elements with which the pupil can continue to form interesting figures in the already well-known manner Figs 11 and 12, on Plate XL, are such fundamental forms, the development of which to other figures will give rise to many instructive remarks These figures show us that for such formations the horizontal as well as the perpendicular line may have the double length Fig 11 shows the horizontal lines combined in such a way as if to form an acute angled triangle They, however, form a right angled triangle, only the right angle is not, as heretofore, at the end of the longest line, but where ? An acute-

angled triangle would result if the horizontal lines were all two net squares distant from each other Then, however, the perpendicular lines would form an obtuse-angled triangle

Important progress is made, when we combine horizontal and perpendicular lines in such a way that by touching in two points they form closed figures, squares and oblongs

First, the child draws squares of one-length's dimension, then of two lengths, of three, four and five lines These are combined then as perpendicular lines were combined also 1^2 with 2^2, the 1^2, 2^2, and 3^2, etc These combinations can be carried out in a perpendicular direction, when the squares will stand over or under each other ; or in horizontal, when the squares will stand side by side ; or, finally, these two opposites may be combined with one another

Fig 13^a shows as an example a combination of four squares in a horizontal direction ; 13^b is the opposite ; c and d are forms of mediation

In Fig 14^a, squares of the first, second and third sizes are combined perpendicularly and horizontally, forming a right angle to the right below ; b is the opposite. (angle left above,) c and d are forms of mediation The same rule is followed here as with the right angle formed by single lines The simple elements are combined with each other into a square with full or hollow middle, etc , and from the new elements thus produced larger figures are again created, as the example Fig 15, Plate XLI , illustrates From the four elements 14^{abcd}, the figure 15^a and its opposite B are constructed, (analogous to the manner employed with Fig 28 Plate XXXVII,) a two fold combination of which resulted in Fig 15 Squares of from one to five length lines of course admit of being combined in similar manner Each essentially new element should give rise to a number of exercises, conditioned only by the individual ability of the child It must be left to the faithful teacher, by an earnest observation and study of her pupils, to find the right extent, here as everywhere in

their occupations Indiscriminate skipping
is not allo ved, neither to pupil nor teacher,
each following production must, under all circumstances be derived from the preceding one

As the square was the result of angles
formed of lines of equal length so also with
the oblong   Here too the child begins with
the simplest   It forms oblongs, the base of
which is a single line, the height of which is a
line of double length   It reverses the case
then   Base line 2, height single length   Re-
taining the same proportions, it progresses to
larger oblongs the height of which is double
the size of its base, and vice versa until it
has reached the numbers 5 and 10

It is but natural that these oblongs, standing or lying should also be united in perpendicular, and horizontal directions   Each form
thus produced again assumes four different
positions, and the four elements are again
united to new formations, according to the
rules previously explained   Fig 16ª shows an
arrangement of standing oblongs, in horizontal
directions   The opposite would contain the
right angle, at a to the right below—to the
left above, 16ᶜ would be one form of mediation, a second one, (opposite of 16ᶜ) would
have its right angle to the right above

Fig 17 shows a combination of lying oblongs, in a perpendicular direction   Fig 18,
shows oblongs in perpendicular and horizon
tal directions   Fig 19, a combination of stand
ing and lying oblongs, the former being ar
ranged perpendicularly, the latter, horizon
tally

In Fig 20, we find standing oblongs so
combined that the form represents an acute
angled triangle, a and b are the only possible
opposites in the same

These few examples may suffice to indicate
the abundance of forms which may be con
structed with such simple material as the
horizontal and perpendicular lines, from 1 to
5 lengths, (and double)

It is the task of the educator to lead the
learner to detect the elements, logically, in
order to produce with them, new forms in

unlimited numbers, within the boundaries of
the laws laid down for this purpose

But even without using these elements the
child will be able owing to continued practice,
to represent manifold forms of life and beauty,
partly by its own free invention, partly by
imitating the objects it has seen before   As
samples of the former, Plate XLII, Fig 27,
shows a cross, Fig 29, a triumphal gate, Fig
30 a wind mill, of the latter, Fig 21—24, and
28, show samples of borders, Fig 25 and 26,
show other simple embellishments   As the
perpendicular line conditioned its opposite,
the horizontal line, both again condition their
mediation

THE OBLIQUE LINE
(PLATES XLIII TO XLV)

Our remarks here can be brief as the ope
rations are nothing but a repetition of those
in connection with the perpendicular line

The child practices the drawing of lines
from 1 to 5 lengths, (Plate XLIII, 1 to 5,)
and combines these, receiving thereby 4 op
positionally equal right angled triangles, (Fig
6—9,) of which it produces a square, (Fig 10)
its opposite (Fig 11) forms of mediation, and
finally large figures

Then the lines are arranged into obtuse
angles and the same process gone through
with them

With these, as in Fig 13, its opposite 16,
and its forms of mediation, 14 and 15, the
obtuse angles will be found at the perpendic
ular middle line, or as in 17, at the horizontal
middle line   By a combination of 15 and 17,
we produce a star, 19   Finally we have also,
reached here the formation of the acute
angled triangle, (Fig 18)   The oblique line
presents particular richness in forms, as it
may be a line of various degrees of inclina
tion   It is an oblique of the first degree
whenever it appears as the diagonal of a
square, as in Figs 1—19   When it appears
as the diagonal of an oblong, it is either an
oblique of the 2d, 3d 4th or 5th degree, ac
cording to the proportions of the base line.

and height of the oblong, 1 to 2, 1 to 3, 1 to 4, 1 to 5

In Fig 20ᵃ, obliques of the second degree are united to a right angled triangle 20ᵇ is the opposite, 20ᶜ and *d* form mediations

In Fig 21, the same lines are united in an obtuse angled triangle In Fig 22, they finally form an acute angle

In all these cases, the obliques were diagonals of standing oblongs They may just as well be diagonals of lying oblongs Fig 23, in which obliques from the first to the fifth degree are united, will illustrate this The obliques are here arranged one above the other In Fig 24, the members *a* and *b* show a similar combination, the obliques, however, are arranged beside one another, the members, *c* and *d*, are formed of diagonals of standing oblongs

Obliques of various grades can be united with one point, when the element *a* in Fig 25, will be produced, which requires the other elements, *b*, *c*, and *d*, to form this figure, the opposite of which would have to be formed according to the formula, $\dfrac{b \mid d}{c \mid a}$, beside which the forms of mediation would appear as $\dfrac{c \mid a}{b \mid d}$ (Fig. 26) and $\dfrac{d \mid b}{a \mid c}$

As in this case, lying figures are produced, standing ones can be produced likewise Each two of the elements thus received may be united, so that all obliques issue from one point, as in Fig 27, and in its opposite, Fig 28

An oppositional combination can also take place, so that each two lines of the same grade meet, (Fig 29) The combination of obliques with obliques to angles, to squares and oblongs now follow, analogous to the method of combining oblongs, perpendicular and horizontal lines Finally the combination of perpendicular and oblique, horizontal and oblique lines to angles, rhombus and rhomboid is introduced

With these, the child tries his skill in pro-

ducing forms of life Fig 40, gate of a fortress, 41, church with school house and cemetery wall, and forms of beauty Figs 30—39 The task of the Kinder Garten and the teacher has been accomplished if the child has learned to manage oblique lines of the first and second degree skillfully All given instruction which aimed at something beyond this was intended for the study of the teacher and the Primary Department, which is still more the case in regard to—

THE CURVED LINE
(PLATE XLVI)

Simply to indicate the progress, and to give Froebel's system of instruction in drawing complete, we add the following and Plate XLVI in illustration of it

First, the child has to acquire the ability to draw a curved line The simplest curved line is the circle, from which all others may be derived

However, it is difficult to draw a circle and the net on slate and paper do not afford sufficient help and guide for so doing But on the other hand, the child has been enabled to draw squares, straight and oblique lines, and with the assistance of these it is not difficult to find a number of points which lie on the periphery of a circle of given size

It is known that all corners of a quadrangle (square or oblong) lie in the periphery of a circle whose diameter is the diagonal of the quadrangle In the same manner all other right angles constructed over the diameter, are periphery angles, affording a point of the desired circular line It is therefore necessary to construct such right angles, and this can be done very readily with the assistance of obliques of various grades

Suppose we draw from point *a* (Fig 1) an oblique of the third degree, as the diagonal of a standing oblong, draw then, starting from point *c*, an oblique of the third degree as diagonal of a lying oblong, and continue both these lines They will meet in point *a*, and there form a right angle

All obliques of the same degree, drawn from opposite points, will do the same as soon as the one approaches the perpendicular in the same proportion in which the other comes near the horizontal, or as soon as the one is the diagonal of a standing the other of a lying oblong

The lines *Aa* and *Cc* are obliques of the third, *Ab* and *Cb* of the second, *Af* and *Cf* of the third degree, etc, etc   In this manner it is easy to find a number of points, all of which are points in the circular line, intended to be drawn   Two or three of them over each side, will suffice to facilitate the drawing of the CIRCUMscribing circle, (Fig 2)   In like manner, the INTERscribing circle will be obtained by drawing the middle transversals of the square, (Fig 3,) and constructing from their end points angles in the previously described manner

After the pupil has obtained a correct idea of the size and form of the circle, whose radius may be of from one to five lengths, it will divide the same in half and quarter circles, producing thereby the elements for its farther activity

The course of instruction is here again the same as that in connection with the perpendicular line   The pupil begins with quarter circles, radius of which is of a single length   Then follow quarter circles with a radius of from two to five lengths   By arrangement of these five quarter circles, four elements are produced, which are treated in the same manner as the triangles produced by arrangement of five straight lines   The segments may be parallel, and the arrangement may take place in perpendicular and horizontal direction, (Fig 4 and 5,) or they may, like the obliques of various degrees, meet in one point, as in Fig 8, of which Figs 4 and 5 are examples

Fig 6 represents the combination of the elements *a* and *d* as a new element , Fig 7, the combination of *d* and *c*   In Fig 8 the arrangement finally takes place in oblique direction, and all lines meet in one point

The quarter circle is followed by the half circle 9 10, 11 , then the three fourths circle (Fig 12), and the whole circle, as shown in Fig 13

With the introduction of each new line, the same manner of proceeding is observed

Notwithstanding the brevity with which we have treated the subject, we nevertheless believe we have presented the course of instruction in drawing sufficiently clearly and forcibly, and hope that by it we have made evident

1   That the method described here is perfectly adapted to the child's abilities, and fit to develop them in the most logical manner ,

2   That the abundance of mathematical perceptions offered with it, and the constant necessity for combining according to certain laws, can not fail to surely exert a wholesome influence in the mental development of the pupil ,

3   That the child thus prepared for future instruction in drawing, will derive from such instruction more benefit than a child prepared by any other method.

Whosoever acknowledges the importance of drawing for the future life of the pupil— may he be led therein by its significance for industrial purposes, or æsthetic enjoyment, which latter it may afford even the poorest !— will be unanimous with us in advocating an early commencement of this branch of instruction with the child

If there be any skeptics on this point, let them try the experiment, and we are sure they will be won over to our side of the question

THE ELEVENTH AND TWELFTH GIFTS.

——— • • ———

MATERIAL FOR PERFORATING AND EMBROIDERING

(PLATES XLVII TO I)

IT is claimed by us that all occupation ma terial presented by Froebel in the Gifts of the Kinder-Garten, are, in some respects, related to each other complementing one another What logical connection is there between the occupation of perforating and embroidering, introduced with the present and the use of the previously introduced Gifts of the Kinder Garten ? This question may be asked by some superficial enquirer Him we answer thus In the first Gifts of the Kinder Garten, the *solid mass of bodies* prevailed , in the fol-lowing ones the *plane*, then the *embodied line* was followed by the *drawn* line, and the occu pation here introduced brings us down to the *point* With the introduction of the per-forating paper and pricking needle, we have descended to the *smallest part of the whole—* the *extreme limit of mathematical divisibility*, and in a playing manner, the child followed us unwittingly, on this, in an abstract sense, difficult journey

The material for these occupations is a piece of net paper, which is placed upon some layers of soft blotting paper The pricking or perforating tool is a rather strong sewing needle, fastened in a holder so as to project about one fourth of an inch Aim of the occupation is the production of the beau-tiful, not only by the child's own activity, but by its own invention Steadiness of the eye and hand are the visible results of the occu pation which directly prepares the pupil for various kinds of manual labor The per-forating, accompanied by the use of the

needle and silk, or worsted, in the way em broidery is done, it is evident in what direc-tion the faculty of the pupil may be developed

The method pursued with this occupation is analogous to that employed in the drawing department Starting from the single point, the child is gradually led through all the various grades of difficulty , and from step to step its interest in the work will increase, especially as the various colors of the em-broidered figures add much to their liveliness, as do the colored pencils in the drawing department

The child first pricks perpendicular lines of two and three lengths, then of four and five lengths, (Figs 2 and 3) They are united to a triangle, opposites and forms of mediation are found, and these again are united into squares with hollow and filled middle, (Figs 4 and 5) The horizontal line follows, (Figs 6—8,) then the combination of perpendicu-lar and horizontal to a right angle in its four oppositionally equal positions, (Figs 9—12) The combination of the four elements present a vast number of small figures If the exter nal point of the angle of 9 and 10 touch one another, the cross (Fig 13) is produced , if the end points of the legs of these figures touch, the square is made. (Fig 14) By repeatedly uniting 9 and 12 Fig 15 is pro-duced, and by the combination of all four angles Figs 16 and 17 According to the rules followed in laying figures with tab lets of Gift Seven, and in drawing, or by a simple application of the law of opposites, the

child will produce a large number of other
figures

The combination of lines of 1 and 2 lengths
is then introduced, and standing and lying
oblongs are formed, (Figs 18 and 19,) etc
The school of perforating *per se*, has to con
sider still simple squares and lying and
standing oblongs, consisting of lines of from
2 to 5 lengths In order no. to repeat the
same form too often, we introduce in Figs
21—31 a series of less simple , containing,
however, the fundamental forms, showing in
the meantime the combination of lines of
various dimensions

In a similar way, the oblique line is now
introduced and employed The child pricks
it in various directions commencing with a
one length line, (Figs 32—35) combines it to
angles, (Figs 36—39,) the combination of
which will again result in many beautiful
forms Then follows the perforating of oblique lines of from 2 to 5 lengths, (a single
length containing up to seven points,) which
are employed for the representation of bor
ders, corner ornaments, etc , (Figs 42—45.
61) The oblique of the second degree is
also introduced, as shown in Figs 46 and 47,
and the peculiar formations in Figs 48—51

Finally, the combination of the oblique
with the perpendicular line, (Figs 52 and 54,)
and with the horizontal, (Figs 53 and 55,) or
with both at the same time, (Figs 56—60,),
takes place The conclusion is arrived at in
the circle (Fig 62) and the half circle (Figs
63—69)

All these elements may be combined in
the most manifold manner, and the inventive
activity of the pupil will find a large field in
producing samples of borders, corner pieces,
frames, reading marks, etc , etc

When it is intended to produce anything of
a more complicated nature, the pattern should
be drafted by pupil or teacher upon the net
paper previous to pricking In such cases,
it is advisable and productive of pleasure to
the pupils, if beneath the perforating paper
another one doubly folded is laid, to have the

pattern transferred by perforation upon this
paper in various copies. Such little productions may be used for various purposes, and
be presented by the children to their friends
on many occasions To assist the pupils in
this respect, it is recommended that simple
drawings be placed in the hands of the pupils,
which, owing to their little ability, they certainly could not yet produce by drawing, but
which they can well trace with their perforating tool These drawings should represent objects from the animal and vegetable
kingdoms, and may thus be of great service
for the mental development of the children
The slowly and carefully perforated forms
and figures will undoubtedly be more lastingly impressed upon the mind and longer
retained by the memory, than if they were
only described or hurriedly looked at Plate
XLIX presents a few of such pictures, which
can easily be multiplied

A particular explanation is required for
Fig 84, on Plate L In this figure are con
tained shaded parts, indicating plastic forms
which so far have not been introduced, all
previous figures presenting mere outlines to
be perforated It is supposed to be known
that each prick of the needle causes some
what of an elevation on the reverse (wrong
side) of the paper If a number of very fine,
scarcely visible pricks are made around a
certain point, an elevated place will be the
result, so much more observable, the larger
the number of pricks concentrated on the
spot In this wise it is possible to represent
certain parts of a design as standing out in
relief It is understood that very young chil
dren could not well succeed in such kind of
work The older ones find material in Figs
72, 74 and 76 to try their skill in this direction, and thereby prepare themselves for figures like 84

All figures of Plates XXXIX , XLII , and
XLIX may well be used for samples of perforating and embroidering

It should be mentioned that the embroidering does not begin simultaneously with the

perforating, but only after the children have
acquired considerable skill in the last named
occupation. For purposes of

EMBROIDERING,

The same net paper which was used for exercises in perforating may be employed, by fill-
ing out the intervals between the holes with
threads of colored silk or worsted. It will be
sufficient for this purpose to combine the
points of one net square only, because otherwise the stitches would become too short to
be made with the embroidery needle in the
hands of children yet unskilled. For work to
be prepared for a special purpose, the perforated pattern should be transferred upon stiff
paper or bristol board

Course of instruction just the same as with
perforating

Experience will show that of the figures
contained on our plates, some are more fit for
perforating, others better adapted for embroidering. Either occupation leads to peculiar
results. Figures in which strongly rounded
lines predominate may be easily perforated,
but with difficulty or not at all be embroid-
ered as Figs 75 and 77. By the process of
embroidering, however, plain forms, as stars,
and rosettes, are easily produced, which could
hardly be represented, or, at best very imper-
fectly only, by the perforating needle. Figs
87—92 and Fig 39 on Plate XLII are examples of this kind

To develop the sense of color in the children, the paper on which they embroider,
should be of all the various shades and hues,
through the whole scale of colors. If the
paper is gray blue, black, or green, let the
worsted or silk be of a rose color, white, or-
ange or red, and if the pupil is far enough
advanced to represent objects of nature, as
fruit, leaves, plants, or animals, it will be very
proper to use in embroidering, the colors

shown by these natural objects. Much can
be thereby accomplished toward an early development of appreciation and knowledge of
color, in which grown people, in all countries
are often sadly deficient. It has appeared to
some as if this occupation is less useful than
pleasurable. Let them consider that the ordi
nary seeing of objects already is a difficult
matter, nay, really an art, needing long practice. Much more difficult and requiring much
more careful exercise, is a true and correct
perception of color

If the *beautiful* is introduced at all as a
means of education—and in Froebel's institutions it occupies a prominent place—it should
approach the child in various ways; not only
in *form*, but in *color*, and *tone* also. To insure
the desired result in this direction, we begin
in the Kinder Garten, where we can much
more readily make impressions upon the
blank minds of children, than at a later period when other influences have polluted their
tastes

For this reason, we go still another step
farther, and give the more developed pupil a
box with the three fundamental colors, showing him their use, in covering the perforated
outlines of objects with the paint. Children
like to occupy themselves in this manner, and
show an increased interest, if they first produce the drawing and are subsequently allowed to use the brush for further beautifying
their work

We only give three fundamental colors, in
order not to confound the beginner by need
less multiplicity, as also to teach how the sec
ondary colors may be produced by mixing the
primary.

The perforating and embroidering are begun with the children in the Kinder-Garten,
when they have become sufficiently prepared
for the perception of forms by the use of their
building blocks and staffs

THE THIRTEENTH GIFT

——•‧•——

MATERIAL FOR CUTTING PAPER AND MOUNTING PIECES TO PRODUCE FIGURES AND FORMS

(PLATES LI TO LVIII)

THE labor, or occupation alphabet, pie sented by Froebel in his system of education, cannot spare the occupation, now introduced —the cutting of paper—the transmutation of the material by division of its parts, notwith standing the many apparently well founded doubts, whether scissors should be placed into the hands of the child at such an early age It will be well for such doubters to consider Firstly, that the scissors which the children use, have no sharp points but are rounded at their ends, by which the possibilities of doing harm with them are greatly reduced Sec ondly, it is expected that the teacher employs all possible means to watch and superintend the children with the utmost care during their occupation with the scissors Thirdly, as it can never be prevented that at least, at times scissors knives and similar dangerous objects may fall into the hands of children it is of great importance to accustom them to such, by a regular course of instruction in their use, which, it may be expected will certainly do something to prevent them from illegitimately applying them for mischievous purposes

By placing material before them from which the child produces, by cutting according to certain laws, highly interesting and beautiful forms, their desire of destroying with the scis sors will soon die out, and they, as well as their parents, will be spared many an unpleas ant experience, incident upon this childish in stinct, if it were left entirely unguided

As material for the cutting we employ a square piece of paper of the size of one six teenth sheet, similar to the folding sheet Such a sheet is broken diagonally, (Plate LXIX, Fig 5) the right acute angle placed upon the left, so as to produce four triangles resting one upon another Repeating the same proceeding, so that by so doing the two upper triangles will be folded upwards, the lower ones downwards in the halving line, eight triangles resting one upon another, will be produced, which we use as our first funda mental form *This fundamental form is held, in all exercises, so that the open side where no plane connects with another is always turned toward the left*

In order to accomplish a sufficient exact ness in cutting the uppermost triangle con tains, (or if it does not, is to be provided with) a kind of net as a guide in cutting Dotted lines indicate on our plates this net work

The activity itself is regulated according to the law of opposites We commence with the perpendicular cut come to its opposite, the horizontal and finally to the mediation of both, the oblique

Plates 51—53 indicate the abundance of cuts which may be developed according to this method and it is advisable to arrange for the child a selection of the simpler elements into a school of cutting

The following selection presents, almost always two opposites and their combination, or leaves out one of the former as is the case with the horizontal cut, wherever it does not produce anything essentially new

a Perpendicular cuts, 2 3, 4—5 6, 7

b Horizontal cuts, 8 9—(above, above and below).

c Perpendicular and horizontal, 18, 19, 20—21, 22, 23

d Oblique cuts, 34, 35—36, 37, 38

e Oblique and perpendicular, 51, 52, 53, —54 55, 56—58, 59, 60

f Oblique and horizontal 65, 66, 67

g Half oblique cuts where the diagonals of standing and lying oblongs, formed of two net squares serve as guides—117, 118, 119—121 122, 123—125, 126, 127

Here ends the school of cutting, *per se*, for the first fundamental form, the right angled triangle The given elements may be combined in the most manifold manner, as this has been sufficiently carried out in the forms on our plates

The fundamental form used for Plates LIV and LV is a *six fold equilateral triangle* It also is produced from the folding sheet, by breaking it diagonally, halving the middle of the diagonal, dividing again in three equal parts the angle situated on this point of halving The angles thus produced will be angles of 60 degrees The leaf is folded in the legs of these angles by bending the one acute angle of the original triangle, upwards the other downwards By cutting the protruding corners, we shall have the desired form of the six fold equilateral triangle, in which the entirely open side serves as basis of the triangle. The net for guidance is formed by division of each side in four equal parts, uniting the points of division of the base, by parallel lines with the sides, and drawing of a perpendicular from the upper point of the triangle upon its base It is the oblique line, particularly which is introduced here The designs and patterns from 133—145, will suffice for this purpose The same fundamental form is used for practising and performing the circular cuts, although the right angular fundamental form may be used for the same purpose Both find their application subsequently in a sphere of development only after the child by means of the use of the half and whole rings, and

drawing has become more familiar with the curved line These exercises require great facility in handling the scissors, besides, and are, therefore, only to be introduced with children, who have been occupied in this department quite a while For such it is a capital employment and they will find a rich field for operation, and produce many an interesting and beautiful form in connection with it The course of development is indicated in figures 164—172

After the child has been sufficiently introduced into the cutting school, in the manner indicated in the above, after his fantasy has found a definite guidance in the ever-repeated application of the law, which protects him against unbounded option and choice, it will be an easy task to him, and a profitable one, to pass over to free invention, and to find in it a fountain of enjoyment, ever new, and inexhaustibly overflowing To let the child, entirely without a guide, be the master of his own free will, and to keep all discipline out of his way, is one of the most dangerous and most foolish principles to which a misunderstood love of children, alone, could bring us. This absolute freedom condemns the children, too soon, to the most unsupportable annoyance All that is in the child should be brought out by means of external influence To limit this influence as much as possible is not to suspend it Froebel has limited it, in a most admirable way by placing this guidance into the child itself, as early as possible, that from one single incitement issues a number of others, within the child, by accustoming it to a lawful and regulated activity from its earliest youth

With the first perpendicular cut, which we made into the sheet (Fig 1,) the whole course of development, as indicated in the series of figures up to No 132 is given, and all subsequent inventions are but simple natural combinations of the element presented in the *"school"* Thus a logical connection prevails in these formations, as among all other means of education, hardly any but mathematics may afford

Whereas the activity of the cutting itself, the logical progress in it advances a most beneficial influence upon the intellect of the pupil, the results of it will awaken his sense of beauty, his taste for the symmetrical, his appreciation of harmony in no less degree The simplest cut already yields an abundance of various figures If we make as in Fig 5, Plate LI, two perpendicular cuts, and unfold all single parts, we shall have a square with hollow middle, a small square and finally the frame of a square If we cut according to Fig 6, we produce a large octagon, four small triangles, four strips of paper of a trapezium form, nine figures altogether

All these parts are now symmetrically arranged according to the law union of opposites—here effected by the position or direction of the parts, relative to the center—and after they have been arranged in this manner, the pupils will often express the desire to preserve them in this arrangement This natural desire finds its gratification by

MOUNTING THE FIGURES

As separation always requires its opposite, uniting, so the cutting requires mounting Plates LVI to LVIII present some examples from which the manner in which the results of the cutting may be applied, can be easily derived With the simpler cuts, the clippings are to be employed, but if a main figure is complete and in accordance with the claims of beauty in itself, it would be foolish to spoil it, by adding the same

This occupation, also, can be made subservient to influence the intellectual development of the child by requiring it to point out all manners in which these forms may be arranged and put together (Plate LVI, Fig 5)

In order to increase the interest of the children, to give a larger scope to their inventive power, and at the same time, to satisfy their taste and sense of color, they may have paper of various colors and be allowed to exchange their productions among one another

Both these occupations, cutting and mounting, are for Kinder Garten as well as higher grades of schools For older pupils, the cutting out of animals, plants and other forms of life will be of interest, and silhouettes even may be prepared by the most expert

It is evident that not only as a simple means of occupation for the children, during their early life, but as a preparation for many an occupation in real life, the cutting of paper and mounting the parts to figures, as introduced here, are of undeniable benefit

The main object however, is here, as in all other occupations in the Kinder Garten, development of the sense of beauty, as a preparation for subsequent performance in and enjoyment of art

THE FOURTEENTH GIFT

MATERIAL FOR BRAIDING OR WEAVING

(PLATES LIX. TO LXIV)

BRAIDING is a favorite occupation of children The child instinctively, as it were, likes everything contributing to its mental and bodily development, and few occupations may claim to accomplish both, better than the occupation now introduced It requires great care but the three year old child may already see the result of such care, whereas even from twelve to fourteen years old pupils often have to combine all their ingenuity and perseverance to perform certain more complicated tasks in the braiding or weaving department It does not develop the right hand alone, the left also finds itself busy most of the time It satisfies the taste of color, because to each piece of braiding, strips of at least two different colors belong It excites the sense of beauty because beautiful, *i e*, symmetrical, forms are produced ; at least their production is the aim of this occupation The sense and appreciation of number are constantly nourished, nay, it may be asserted, that there is hardly a better means of affording perceptions of numerical conditions, so thorough, founded on individual experience and rendered more distinct by diversity in form and color, than "*braiding*" The products of the child's activity, besides, are readily made useful in practical life, affording thereby capital opportunities for expression of its love and gratitude, by presents prepared by its own hand

The material used for this occupation are sheets of paper prepared as shown on Plate LIX , strips of paper and the braiding needle, also represented on Plate LIX

A braid work is produced by drawing with the needle a loose strip (white) through the strips of the braiding sheet, (green) so that a number of the latter will appear over, another under the loose strip These numbers are conditioned by the form the work is to assume As there are but two possible ways in which to proceed, either lifting up, or pressing down, the strips of the braiding sheet, the course to be taken by the loose strip is easily expressed in a simple formula All varieties of patterns are expressible in such formulas and therefore easily preserved and communicated

The simplest formula of course, is when one strip is raised and the next pressed down We express this formula by 1 *u* (up), 1 *d* (down) All such formulas in which only two figures occur, are called simple formulas ,

combination formulas, however, are such as contain a combination of two or more such simple formulas

But with a single one of such formulas, no braid work can yet be constructed If we should, for instance, repeat with a second, third, and fourth strip, 1 *u*, 1 *d*, the loose strips would slip over one another at the slightest handling, and the strips of the braiding sheet and the whole work, drop to pieces if we should cut from it, the margin In doing the latter, we have, even with the most perfect braidwork, to employ great care ; but it is only then a braid or weaving work exists —when all strips are joined to the whole by other strips, and none remain entirely detached

To produce a braid work, we need at least two formulas, which are introduced alternately Proceeding according to the same fundamental law which has led us thus far in all our work, we combine first with 1 *u*, 1 *d*, its opposite 1 *d*, 1 *u*

Such a combination of braiding formulas by which not merely a single strip, but the whole braid work, is governed, is a *braiding scheme*

Braiding formulas, according to which the single strip moves are easily invented Even if one would limit one's self to take up or press down no more than five strips, (and such a limitation is necessary, because otherwise the braiding would become too loose,) the following thirty formulas would be the result

1, 1u 1d	9, 3u 1d	17, 4u 2d	24, 5d 1u
2, 1d 1u	10, 3d 1u	18, 4d 2u	25, 5u 2d
3, 2u 2d	11, 3u 2d	19, 4u 3d	26, 5d 2u
4, 2d 2u	12, 3d 2u	20, 4d 3u	27, 5u 3d
5, 2u 1d	13, 4u 4d	21, 5u 5d	28, 5d 3u
6, 2d 1u	14, 4d 4u	22, 5d 5u	29, 5u 4d
7, 3u 3d	15, 4u 1d	23, 5u 1d	30, 5d 4u
8, 3d 3u	16 4d 1u		

From these thirty formulas, among which are always two oppositionally alike, as for instance, 1 and 2, 9 and 10, 25 and 26, hundreds of combined or combination formulas can be formed by simply uniting two of them In the beginning it is advisable to combine such as contain equally named numbers either even or odd The following are some examples

Formulas 1 and   3, 1u 1d, 2u 2d
    "   1 and   5 1u 1d, 2u 1d
    "   1 and   7, 1u 1d, 3u 3d
    "   1 and   9, 1u 1d, 3u 1d
    "   1 and 11, 1u 1d, 3u 2d.
    "   1 and 13 1u 1d, 4u 4d
    "   1 and 15, 1u 1d, 4u 1d
    "   1 and 17, 1u 1d, 4u 2d
    "   1 and 19, 1u 1d, 4u 3d
    "   1 and 21, 1u 1d, 5u 5d
    "   1 and 23, 1u 1d, 5u 1d
    "   1 and 25, 1u 1d, 5u 2d
    "   1 and 27, 1u 1d, 5u 3d
    "   1 and 29, 1u 1d, 5u 4d

If we also add the formulas under the even numbers in the given thirty, we have to read them inversely Thus

Formulas 1 and   6, 1u 1d, 1u 2d.
    "   1 and 10, 1u 1d, 1u 3d
    "   1 and 12, 1u 1d, 2u 3d
    "   1 and 16, 1u 1d, 1u 4d
    "   1 and 18, 1u 1d, 2u 4d
    "   1 and 20, 1u 1d, 3u 4d
    "   1 and 24, 1u 1d, 1u 5d
    "   1 and 26, 1u 1d, 2u 5d
    "   1 and 28, 1u 1d, 3u 5d
    "   1 and 30, 1u 1d, 4u 5d

By a combination of one single formula with the twenty four others, we receive new combination formulas and see that inventing formulas is a simple mathematical operation, regulated by the laws of combination

Much more difficult it is to invent *braiding schemes* Not to dwell too long on this point, we introduce the reader to the course shown in pictures on our plates, which is arranged so systematically that either as a whole or with some omissions, it may be worked through with children from three to six years, as a *braiding school* It begins with simple formulas and by means of the law of opposites is carried out to the most beautiful figures

Formula 1, 1u 1d, (Fig 1,) is first introduced , opposite in regard to number is 2u 2d (Fig 2) In Fig 3 the numbers 1 and 2 are combined , Fig 4 is a combination of Figs. 1 and 2 , Fig 5 a combination of Figs

1 and 3 by combining the simple formulas If we examine Fig 5, the number 3 makes itself prominent in the strips running obliquely In Fig 6 it occurs independently as opposite to 1 and 2, and then follows in Figs 7–15 a series of mediative forms all uniting the opposites in regard to number In all these patterns the squares or oblongs produced are arranged perpendicularly under, or horizontally beside, one another Except in Fig 1, the oblique line appears already beside the horizontal and perpendicular Thus, this given opposite *of form* is prevailing on Plate LXI , and we apply here the same formulas as on Plate LX , with the difference, however, that we need only one formula, which in the second, third strip, etc , always begins one strip later or earlier Thus in Fig 16, the formula 2u 2d (as in Fig 2) is carried out The dark and light strips of the pattern run here from right above to left below Opposite of position to Fig 16, is shown in Fig 17, where both run the opposite way Fig. 18 shows combination, and Fig 19 double combination In opposition to the connected oblique lines, the broken line appears in Fig 20 As the formula 2u 2d has furnished us five patterns, so the formula of Fig 3, 1u 2d, furnishes the series 21—25 Nos 21 and 22 are opposites as to direction Fig 23 shows the combination of these opposites Figs 24 and 25, opposites to one another are forms of mediation between 21 and 22 With them for the first time a middle presents itself

While in Figs 21—26 the dark color is prevailing, Figs 26—28 show us predominantly, the light strip, consequently the opposite *in color* In 29—32, formulas from Figs 3—5 are employed Fig 29 requires an opposite of *direction*, a pattern in which the strips run from left above to right below Fig 30 gives the combination of both directions and Figs 31 and 32 are at the same time opposites as to direction and color

It is obvious that each single formula can be used for a whole series of divers patterns, and the invention of these patterns is so easy that it will suffice if we introduce each new formula very briefly

Fig 33 is a form of mediation for the formula 3u 3d , Fig 34 shows a different application of the same formula In Fig 35 the broken line appears again, but in opposition to 20, it changes its direction with each break In Figs 36—40 the formulas of Figs 7, 8, 10, 11, and 13 are carried out The braiding school *per se*, is here concluded Whoever may think it too extensive may select from it Nos 1 2, 3 6, 7, 10, 16, 17, 18, 21, 26, 24, 25, 33 and 34

But if any one would like still to enlarge upon it she may do so by working out, for each single formula the forms or patterns 16, 17 18 19, 24 and 25 and continue the school to the number 5 The number of patterns will be made, thereby, ten times larger

Another change, and enlargement of the school may be introduced by cutting the braiding strips as well as those of the braiding sheet, of different widths We can thereby, represent quite a number of patterns after the same formula, which are, however, essentially different This is particularly to be recommended with very small children, who necessarily will have to be occupied longer with the simple formula 1u 1d But for more developed braiders, such change is of interest, because by it a great variety of forms may be produced which may be rendered still more interesting and attractive, by a variety of colors in the loose braiding strips

With patterns that have a middle, as 24 and 28, it is advisable to let the braiding begin (especially with beginners,) with the middle strip, and then to insert always one strip above, and one below it.

It is not unavoidably necessary that the school should be finished from beginning to end, as given here Quite the reverse The pupil, after having successfully produced some patterns, may be afforded an opportunity for developing his skill by his own invention, in trying to form, by braiding a cross, with hollow middle, (Fig 41,) a standing oblong (42,) a long cross, (43.) a small window, (45) etc

Plate LXIII , presents some patterns which may be used for wall baskets, lamp tidies, book-marks, etc, and which may easily be augmented by such as have acquired more than ordinary skill

Finally, Plate LXIV shows in figures 1—3, obliquely intertwined strips, representing the so called free braiding, the braiding without braiding sheet This is done in the following manner Cut two or more long strips (Fig 4) of a quarter sheet of colored paper, (green,) and fold to half their length, (Fig 5,) cut then, of differently colored paper, (white,) shorter strips, also fold these to half their length Put the green strips side by side of one another, as shown in Fig 7, so that the closed end of the one strip lies above, and that of the other below, (7a) Then take the white strip, bend it around strip 1, and lead it through strip 2, (Fig 8) The second strip is applied in an opposite way, laying it around 2 and leading it through 1 Employing four instead of two green strips, the book mark, Fig 9, will be the result The protruding ends are either cut or scolloped By introducing strips of different widths, a variety of patterns can also here be produced

Instead of paper, glazed muslin, leather, silk or woolen ribbon, straw and the like may be used as material for braiding

THE FIFTEENTH GIFT.

————•◦•————

THE INTERLACING SLATS

(PLATES LXV AND LXVI)

FROEBEL, in his Gifts of the Kinder-Garten, does not present anything perfectly new   All his means of occupation are the result of care ful observation of the playing child   But he has united them in one corresponding whole , he has invented a method, and by this method presented the possibility of producing an ex haustless treasure of formations which, each influencing the mind of the pupil in its pecu liar way, effect a development most harmoni ous and thorough of all the mental faculties The use of slats for interlacing is an occupa tion already known to our ancestors, and who has not practiced it to some extent in the days of childhood?   But who has ever suc ceeded in producing more than five or six figures with them?   Who has ever derived, from such occupation the least degree of that manual dexterity and mental development, inventive power and talent of combination, which it affords the pupils of the Kinder Gar ten, since Froebel's method has been applied to the material?

Our slats, ten inches long, three eighths of an inch broad and one sixteenth of an inch thick, are made of birch or any tough wood and a dozen of them are sufficient to produce quite a variety of figures   They form as it were the transition from the plane of the tab let to the line of the staffs (Ninth Gift) differ ing, however, from both, in the fact that forms produced by them are not bound to the plane but contain in themselves a sufficient hold to be separated from it

The child first receives *one single slat*   Ex-

amining it, it perceives that it is flexible, that its length surpasses its breadth many times, and again that its thickness is many times less than its breadth

Can the pupil name some objects between which and the slat, there is any similarity?

The rafters under the roof of a house, and in the arms of a wind mill, and the laths of which fences, and certain kinds of gates, and lattice work are made are similar to the slat

The child ascertains that the slat has two long plane sides and two ends   It finds its middle or center point can indicate the upper and lower side of the slat its upper and lower end, and its right and left side   After these preliminaries a second slat is given the child On comparison the child finds them perfectly alike, and it is then led to find the positions which the two slats may occupy to each other They can be laid parallel with each other, so as to touch one another with the whole length of their sides, or they may not touch at all

They can be placed in such positions that their ends touch in various ways, and can be laid crosswise, over or under one another.

With an *additional* slat, the child now con tinues these experiments   It can lay various figures with them, but there is no binding or connecting hold   Therefore as soon as it at tempts to lift its work from the table, it falls to pieces

By the use of *four* slats, it becomes enabled to produce something of a connected whole, but this only is done, when each single slat *comes in contact with at least three other slats*

Two of these should be on one side, the third or middle one should rest on the other side of the connecting slat, so that here again the law of opposites and their mediation is followed and practically demonstrated in every figure

It is not easy to apply this law constantly in the most appropriate manner But this very necessity of painstaking, and the reasoning, without which little success will be attained, is productive of rich fruit in the development of the pupil

The child now places the slat *aa* horizontally upon the table *Bb* is placed across it in a perpendicular direction , *cc* in a slanting direction under *a* and *b*, and *dd* is shoved under *aa* and *over bb* and under *cc*, as shown in Fig 1

This gives a connected form, which will not easily drop apart The child investigates how each single slat is held and supported— it indicates the angles, which were created, and the figures which are bounded by the various parts of the slats

To show how rich and manifold the material for observation and instruction given in this one figure is, we will mention that it contains twenty four angles, of which 8 (1—8) are right, 8 (9—16) acute, and 8 (17—24) obtuse —formed by one perpendicular slat, *bb*, one horizontal, *aa*, one slanting from left above to right below, *cc*, and another slanting from right above to left below, *dd*

Each single slat touches each other slat once , two of them, *aa* and *bb* pass over two and under one and the others, *cc* and *dd*, pass under two and over one of the other slats, by which interlacing three small figures are formed within the large figure, one of which is a figure with two right one obtuse and one acute angle (3, 6, 22 10), and four unequal sides, and two others, one of which is a right angled triangle with two equal sides, and the other is a right angled triangle with no equal sides

By drawing the slats of Fig 1 apart, Fig 2, an acute angled triangle is produced — by drawing them together, Fig 3 results, from

which the acute angled triangle Fig 4, can again be easily formed Each of these figures presents abundant matter for investigation and instructive conversation as shown above in connection with Fig 1

The child now receives a *fifth* slat Suppose we have Fig 2, consisting of four slats —ready before us—we can, by adding the fifth slat easily produce what appears on Plate LXV as Fig 8

If the five slats are disconnected, the child may lay two, perpendicularly at some distance from each other, a third in a slanting position over them from right above to left below and a fourth in an opposite direction, when the two latter will cross each other in their middle By means of the fifth slat the interlacing then is carried out by sliding it from right to left under the perpendicular over the crossing two and again under the other perpendicular slat, and thereby the figure 5 made firm.

By bending the perpendicular slats together, Fig 6 is produced , when the horizontal slat assumes a higher position, a five angled figure appears—one of the slanting slats, however, has to change its position also as shown in Fig 7 In Fig 8, the horizontal slat is moved downward In Fig 9, the original position of the crossing slats is changed , in the triangle, Fig 10, still more, and in Figs 11 and 12, other changes of these slats are introduced

The addition of a sixth slat enables us still further to form other figures from the previous ones—Fig 17 can be produced from 9, 18 from 10 or 11, 22 from 12, and then a following series can be obtained by drawing apart and shoving together as heretofore

Let us begin thus the child lays (Fig 13) two slats horizontally upon the table—two slats perpendicularly over them , a large square is produced A fifth slat horizontally across the middle of the two perpendicular slats, gives two parallelograms and by connecting the sixth slat from above to below with the three horizontal slats so that the middle one is under and the two outside slats over it, the child will have formed four small squares, of equal size

The figures 17 and 18, (triangles) and 19 and 23, (hexagons,) deserve particular attention, because they afford valuable means for mathematical observations

On Plate LXVI we find some few examples of seven intertwined slats, (Figs 25—28,) of eight slats, (Figs 29—36,) of nine slats, (Figs 37—40,) and of ten slats (Figs 41—43)

All we have given in the above are mere hints to enable the teacher and pupil to find more readily by individual application the richness of figures to be formed with this occupation material

It is particularly mathematical forms, regular polygons, (Figs 28, 31 40, 42,) contemplation of divisions, produced by diagonals, etc, planes and proportions of form, which, in *forms of knowledge*, are brought before the eye of the pupil, with great clearness and distinctness, by the interlacing slats

In the meantime, it will afford pleasure to behold the *forms of beauty* as given in Figs 30, 33, 37, nor should the *forms of life* be forgotten, as they are easily produced by a larger number of slats, (Fig 39—a fan, 35 and 36—fences,) by combining the work of several pupils

The figures are not simply to be constructed and to be changed to others, but each of them is to be submitted to a careful investigation by the child, as to its angles, its constituent parts, and their qualities, and the service each individual slat performs in the figure as indicated with Fig 1 on page LXV

The occupation with this material will frequently prove perplexing and troublesome to the pupil, oftentimes he will try in vain to represent the object in his mind

Having almost successfully accomplished the task, one of the slats will glide out from his structure, and the whole will be a mass of ruins   It was the *one slat*, which owing to its dereliction in performing its duty destroyed the figure and prevented all the others from performing theirs

It will not be difficult for the thinking teacher to derive from such an occurrence, the opportunity to make an application to other conditions in life, even within the sphere of the young child, and its companions in and out of school   The character of this occupation does not admit of its introduction before the pupils have spent a considerable time in the Kinder Garten, in which it is only begun and continued in the primary department

---

THE SIXTEENTH GIFT.

THE SLAT WITH MANY LINKS

THIS occupation material, which may be used at almost any grade of development in the Kinder Garten, the primary and higher school departments, is so rich in its applications, that we cannot attempt to describe it extensively nor give illustrations of the various ways in which it can be rendered useful   Suffice it to say, that it may be employed in representing all various kinds of lines, angles and mathematical figures, and that even forms of life and beauty may be presented by it

We have slats with 4 6, 8 and 16 links, which are introduced one after the other when opportunities offer   In placing the first into the hand of the child, we would ask him to unfold all the links of the slat, and to place it upon the table so as to represent a perpendicular, horizontal, and then an oblique line

By bending two of the links perpendicularly, and the two others horizontally, we form a right angle Bending one of the legs of the angle toward, or from the other, we receive the acute and obtuse angles, which grow smaller or larger, the nearer or farther the legs are brought to, or from each other until we reduce the angles to either a perpendicular line of two links' length or a horizontal line of the length of four links

We may then form a square Pushing two opposite corners of it toward each other, and bending the first link so as to cover with it the second, and, by then joining the end of the fourth link to where the first and second are united, we shall form an equilateral triangle (Which other triangle can be formed with this slat, and how?)

The capital letters V, W, N, M, Z and the figure 4 can be easily produced by the children, and many figures be constructed by the teacher in which the pupils may designate the

number and kinds of angles, which they contain, as is done with the movable slats on other occasions

The slats with 6, 8 and 16 links, to be introduced one after the other if used in the manner here indicated, can be rendered exceedingly interesting and instructive to the pupils Their ingenuity and inventive power will find a large field in the occupation with this material if, at times they are allowed to produce figures themselves, of which the more advanced pupils may make drawings and give a description of each orally

It would be needless to enlarge here upon the richness of material afforded by this gift as half an hour's study of and practice with it will convince each thinking teacher fully of the treasure in her hand and certainly make her admire it on account of the simplicity of its application for educational purposes in school and family

THE SEVENTEENTH GIFT.

MATERIAL FOR INTERTWINING

(PLATES LXVII, LXVIII)

INTERTWINING is an occupation similar to that of interlacing Aim of both is representation of plane—outlines In the occupation with the interlacing slats we produced forms, which were to be destroyed again, or whose peculiarities at least, had to be changed to produce something new, here, we produce permanent results There, the material was in every respect a ready one, here, the pupil has to prepare it himself There, hard slats of little flexibility, here, soft paper, easily changed There, production of purely mathematical forms by carefully employing a given material, here, production of similar forms

by changing the material, which forms, however, are forms of beauty

The paper strips, not used when preparing the folding sheets, are used as material, adapted for the present occupation They are strips of white or colored paper, from eight to ten inches long and varying in breadth Each strip is subdivided in smaller strips of three-quarters of an inch wide, which by folding their long sides are transformed to threefold strips of eight to ten inches long and one quarter of an inch wide

The children will not succeed well, in forming regular figures from these strips at first

As the main object of this occupation is to accustom the child to a clean, neat and correct performance of his task, some of the tablets of Gift Seven are given him as patterns to assist him; or the child is led to draw on his slate the three, four, or many cornered forms, and to intertwine his paper strips according to these

First, a right angled isosceles triangle is used for laying around it one of these strips so as to enclose it entirely. We begin with the left cathetus, put the tablet upon the strip, folding it toward the right over the right angle. The break of the paper is well to be pressed down and then the strip is again folded around the acute angle toward the left. Where the hypotenuse (large side) touches the left cathetus (small side), the strip is cut and the ends of the figure there closed by gluing them together by some clean adhesive matter. Care should be taken that the one end of each side be under, the other over, that of the other

Thus the various kinds of triangles, (Figs 1—3,) squares, rhombus, rhomboids etc, are produced

Two like figures are combined, as shown in Figs 4—6. If strips prove to be too short, the child is shown how to glue them together, to procure material for larger and more complicated forms. Thus, it produces, with one long strip, Figs 16, 18, 19, 20, with two long strips, Figs 17, 21. Fig 22 shows the natural size; all others are drawn on a somewhat reduced scale. It cannot be difficult to produce a great variety of similar figures, if one will act according to the motives obtained with and derived from the occupation with the interlacing slats

This occupation admits of still another and very beautiful modification, by not only pinching and pressing the strip where it forms angles, but by folding it to a rosette. This process is illustrated in Figs 7—9. The strip is first pinched toward the right, (Fig 7,) then follows the second pinch downward, (Fig 8,) then a third toward the left, when the one end of the strip is pushed through under the other, (Fig 9)

Here, also, simple triangles, squares, pentagons and hexagons are to be formed, then two like figures combined, and finally more complicated figures produced. (Compare examples given in Figs 10—15)

Whatever issues from the child's hand sufficiently neat and clean and carefully wrought may be mounted on stiff paper or bristol board, and disposed of in many ways

The occupation of intertwining shows plainly how by combination of simple mathematical forms, forms of beauty may be produced. These latter should predominate in the Kinder Garten, and the mathematical are of importance as they present the elements for their construction. The mathematical element of all our occupations is in so far of significance, as the child receives from it impressions of form, but of much more importance is the development of the child's taste for the beautiful, because with it, the idea of the good is developed in the meantime

As the various performances of this occupation cutting, folding and mounting, require a somewhat skilled hand, it is introduced in the upper section of the Kinder Garten only

THE EIGHTEENTH GIFT

————•◦•————

MATERIAL FOR PAPER-FOLDING

(PLATES LXIX TO LXXI)

FROEBEL'S sheet of paper for folding, the simplest and cheapest of all materials of occupation, contains within it a great multitude of instructive and interesting forms. Almost every feature of mathematical perceptions, obtained by means of previous occupations, we again find in the occupation of paper-folding. It is indeed a compendium of elementary mathematics, and has, therefore, very justly and judiciously been recommended as a useful help in the teaching of this science in public schools.

Lines, angles, figures, and forms of all varieties appear before us, after a few moments' occupation with this material. The multitude of impressions, however, should not misguide us; and we should always, and more particularly in this work, be careful to accompany the work of the children with necessary conversation and pleasant entertainment, for the relief of their young minds.

We prepare the paper for folding in the following manner.

Take half a sheet of letter paper, place it upon the table in such a manner as to have the longest sides extend from left to right. Then halve it by covering the upper corners with the lower ones, (Fig 1) Then turn the *now* left and right upper (previously *lower*) corners back, towards the center; invert the paper, turn also the two other corners toward the center, and then we have the form of a trapezium, (Fig 2) Unfolding the sheet at its base line, a hexagon, (Fig 3) will show itself, in which we observe four triangles, of

which two and two lie together, forming a larger triangle. At the base lines of these larger triangles the sheet is again folded, and neatly and accurately cut, severing thereby the two large double, lying triangles from the single and oblong strips of paper.

Each of these triangles we cut through from where the sides of the small triangles touch each other, unfold the small triangles, and we now have four square pieces, and one oblong piece of paper, (Fig. 4) The former we employ for folding, the latter we keep for future use, in the occupations of intertwining, braiding, or weaving.

The child should be accustomed to the strictest care and cleanliness in the cutting as well as the folding.

This is necessary, because paper carelessly folded and cut, will not only render more difficult every following task, nay, make impossible every satisfactory result; especially, should this be the case, because, we do not intend simply to while away our own and the child's precious time, but are engaged in an occupation whose final aim is acquisition of ability to work, and to work well—one of the most important claims human society is entitled to make upon each individual.

The child prepares for himself, in the manner described, a number of folding sheets, and submits them to a series of regular changes, by bending and folding, in consequence of which the fundamental forms are produced, from which sequels of forms of life and beauty are subseqently developed, by means of the law of opposites

On the road to this goal a surprising number of forms of knowledge present themselves

The sheet is now folded once more following the diagonal, (Fig 5,) and will then present, when unfolded, the division of the square in two right-angled isosceles triangles

Folded once more according to the other diagonal, (Fig 6,) and again unfolded, we find each of the large triangles, halved by a perpendicular, (Fig 7) Now the lower corner is bent upon the left, and the right one upon the upper, and the sheet is so folded, that it is divided into equal oblong halves by a transversal The same is done to the opposite transversal, and we have the Fig 9, affording a multitude of mathematical object perceptions

If we now take the lower corner, (Fig 9) bend it exactly toward the center of the sheet and fold it the pentagon, (Fig 10) will be the result We fold the opposite corner in like manner and produce the hexagon, (Fig 11) and finally with the two remaining corners, Fig 12^a is formed containing four triangles, touching one another with their free sides each of them again showing a line halving them in two equal triangles

If we invert 12^a, we have 12^b, a connected square, in which the outlines of eight congruent triangles appear If 12^b is unfolded we shall see beside a multiplication of previous forms parallelograms also If we start from 12^a, fold the corners toward the middle, (Fig 15,) we shall receive a form consisting of double layers of paper, and showing four triangles, under which again, four separate squares are found This is the fundamental form for a series of forms of life (Fig 16)

It is utterly impossible to give a minute description how forms of life may be produced from this fundamental form Practical attempts and occasional observation in the Kinder Garten will be of more assistance than the most detailed illustrations and descrip-

tions Froebel's Manual mentions, among others, the following objects A table-cloth with four hanging corners, a bird, a sail boat, a double canoe, a salt cellar flower, chemise, kite, wind-mill, table, cigar holder, flower pot, looking glass, boat with seats, etc Still richer become the forms of life, if we bend the corners of, the described fundamental form, once more toward the middle In connection with this the manual mentions the following forms the knitting-pouch, the chest of drawers, the boots, the hat, the cross the pantaloons, the frame the gondola, etc For the construction of these forms, it is advisable to use a larger sheet of paper perhaps half a sheet of letter paper

But the simple fundamental form, for the forms of life is also the fundamental form for the forms of beauty, contained on Plate LXX, (Fig 16) Unfold the fundamental form do not press the corners but first the middle of the upper and lower side, then the two other sides toward the middle of the sheet, and the double canoe will be the result (hexagon with two long and four short sides) If the over-reaching triangles are now bent back toward the middle, Fig 17 appears, from which, up to Fig 21 the following forms are easily constructed according to the law of opposites

From quite a similar fundamental form, the series 22—27 originates

If we finally take the sheet as represented, in 12^b fold the lower right corner toward the middle, also the left upper, (Fig 13) also the two remaining corners, we shall have four triangles, consisting of a double layer of paper which may be lifted up from the square ground and which upper layer again is divided in two triangles, (Fig 14)

Invert this figure and you will have Fig 28 four single squares, the fundamental form of a series of forms of beauty on Plate LXXI, the latter easily to be derived from this former, under the guidance of the well known law of opposites

The hints given in the above might be augmented to a considerable extent and still not

exhaust the matter They are given especially to stimulate teacher and child to individual practical attempts in producing forms
by folding The best results of their activity
can be improved by cutting out or coloring,
which adds a new and interesting change to
this occupation A change of the fundamental
form in three directions yields various series
of forms of beauty, which may be multiplied *ad infinitum* Thereby, not only the idea
of sequel in representations is given but also
the understanding unlocked for the various
orders in nature

Furthermore, this occupation gives the pu

pil such manual dexterity as scarcely any
other does, and prepares the way to various
female occupations, besides being immediately
preparatory to all plastic work Early training
in cleanliness and care is also one of the re
sults of a protracted use of the folding sheet
It is evident that only those children who
have been a good while in the Kinder Garten,
can be employed in this department of occupation The peculiar fitness of the folding
sheet for mathematical instruction beyond the
Kinder-Garten, must be apparent after we
have shown how useful it can be made in this
institution

THE NINETEENTH GIFT.

MATERIAL FOR PEAS WORK

(PLATES LXXII AND LXXIII)

WE have already tried, in connection with
the Ninth Gift, (the laying staffs,) to render
permanent the productions of the pupils, by
stitching or pasting them to stiff paper We
satisfied, by so doing a desire of the child,
which grows stronger, as the child grows
older—the desire to produce by his own activity certain lasting results It is no longer the
incipient instinct of activity which governs
the child, the instinct which prompted it, apparently without aim, to destroy everything
and to reconstruct in order to again de
stroy A higher pleasure of production has
taken its place, not satisfied by mere doing,
but requiring for its satisfaction also delight
in the created object—if even unconsciously—
the delight of progress, which manifests itself
in the production, and which can be observed
only in and by the permanency of the object
which enables us to compare it with objects
previously produced

To satisfy the claims of the pupil in this

direction in a high degree, the working with
peas is eminently fitted, although considerable
manual skill is required for it, not to be ex
pected in any child before the fifth year The
material consists of pieces of wire of the thickness of a hair pin, of various sizes in length
and pointed at the ends They again represent
lines As means of combination, as embodied
points of junction, peas are used, soaked about
twelve hours in water and dried one hour pre
vious to being used They are then just soft
enough to allow the child to introduce the
points of the wires into them and also hard
enough to afford a sufficient hold to the latter

The first exercise is to combine two wires,
by means of one pea, into a straight line, an
obtuse, right, and acute angle What has been
said in regard to laying of staffs in connection
with Fig 1—23 on Plate XXX will serve
here also.

Of three wires, a longer line is formed,
angles, with one long, and one short side

The three wires are introduced into one pea, so that they meet in one point, two parallel lines may be continued by a third, finally the equilateral triangle is produced

Then follows the square, parallelogram, rhomboid, diagonals may be drawn and the forms shown on Plate LXXII figures 1—10, be produced   The possibility of representing the most manifold forms of knowledge, of life and of beauty, is reached, and the forms produced may be used for other purposes   The child may produce six triangles of equal size, and repeat with them all the exercises, gone through with the tablets, and may enlarge upon them

Or the child may prepare 4 8, 16 right angled triangles, or obtuse angled, or acute angled triangles and lay with them the figures given on Plate LXXII, etc, for the course of drawing and carry them out still further

After these hints it seems impossible not to occupy the child in an interesting and instructive manner

But the condition attached to each new Gift of the Kinder Garten is some special progress in its course

We produced outlines of many objects with the staffs, all formations, however, remained planes, whose sides were represented by staffs In the working with peas, the wires represent edges, the peas serve as corners, and these skeleton bodies are so much more instructive as they allow the observation of the outer forms in their outlines, and the inner structure and being of the body at the same time.

The child unites two equilateral triangles by three equally long wires and forms thereby a prism, (Fig 14,) four equilateral triangles, give the three sided pyramid, eight of them, the octahedron   (Figs 15 and 16)

From two equal squares, united by four wires of the length of the sides, the skeleton cube, Fig 17, is formed, if the uniting wires are longer than the sides of the square, the four sided column (Fig 8) is one of the squares larger than the other, a topless pyramid will be produced, etc

It is hardly possible that pupils of the Kinder Garten should make any further progress in the formation of these mathematical forms of crystallization, as the representation of the many sided bodies and especially the development of one from another, requires greater care and skill than should be expected at such an early period of life.   It will be reserved for the primary, and even a higher grade of school, to proceed farther on the road indicated and in this manner prepare the pupil for a clear understanding of regular bodies   (Fig 19 shows how the octahedron is contained in the cube)

This, however, does not exclude the construction by the more advanced pupils of the Kinder Garten, of simple objects, in their surroundings, such as benches, (Fig 21,) chairs, (Fig 23,) baskets, etc, or to try to invent other objects

Whoever has himself tried peas work will be convinced of its utility   Great care, much patience, are needed to produce a somewhat complicated object, but a successful structure repays the child for all painstaking and perseverance   By this exercise, the pupils improve in readiness of construction, and this is an important preparation for organization

More advanced pupils try also, successfully to construct letters and numerals, with the material of this Gift

The bodies produced by peas work may be used as models in the modeling department   The one occupation is the complement of the other   The skeleton cube allows the observation of the qualities of the solid cube, in greater distinctness   The image of the body becomes in this manner more perfect and clear, and above all, the child is led upon the road, on which alone it is enabled to come into possession of a true knowledge and correct estimate of things, the road on which it learns, not only to observe the external appearance of things, but in the meantime, and always, to look at their internal being

THE TWENTIETH GIFT.

MATERIAL FOR MODELING

(PLATE LXXIV)

MODELING, or working in clay, held in high estimation by Froebel, as an essential part of the whole of his means of education is, strange to say, much neglected in the Kinder-Garten As the main objection to it named is that the children, even with the greatest care, can not prevent occasionally soiling their hands and their clothes Others, again, believe that an occupation, directly preparing for art, very rarely can be continued in life They call it, therefore, aimless pastime without favorable consequences, either for internal development or external happiness

If it must be admitted that the soiling of the hands and clothing cannot always be avoided, we hold that for this very reason, this occupation is a capital one, for it will give an opportunity to accustom the children to care, order and cleanliness, provided the teacher herself takes care to develop the sense of the pupils, for these virtues, in connection with this occupation, as on all other occasions, she should strive to excite the sense of cleanliness as well as purity Certainly, parts of the adhesive clay will stick to the little fingers and nails of the children, and their wooden knives, but, pray, what harm can grow out of this? The child may learn even from this fact It may be remarked in connection with it, that the callous hand of the husbandman, the dirty blouse of the mechanic, only show the occupation, and cannot take aught from the inner worth of a man As regards the objection to this occupation as aimless and without result, it should be considered that

occupation with the beautiful, even in its crudest beginnings, always bears good fruit, because it prepares the individual for a true appreciation and noble enjoyment of the same Just in this the significance of Froebel's educational idea partly rests, that it strives to open every human heart for the beautiful and good—that it particularly is intended to elevate the social position of the laboring classes by means of education, not only in regard to knowledge and skill but also, in regard to a development of refinement and feeling

Representing, imitating, creating, or transforming in general, is the child's greatest enjoyment Bread crumbs are modeled by it into balls, or objects of more complicated form and even when biting bits from its cooky, it is the child's desire to produce *form* If a piece of wax, putty, or other pliable matter, falls into its hands, it is kneaded until it assumes a form of which they may assert that it represents a baby,—the dog Roamer or what not! Wet sand, they press into their little cooking utensils, when playing "house-keeping," and pass off the forms as puddings, tarts, etc, in one word, most children are born sculptors Could this fact have escaped Froebel's keen observation? He has here provided the means to satisfy this desire of the child, to develop also this talent, in its very awakening

According to Froebel's principle, the first exercises in modeling are the representation of the fourteen stereometric fundamental forms of crystallization, which he presents in a box, by themselves as models Starting from the *cube* the *cylinder* follows—then the *sphere pyramid* with 3 4 and 6 *sides* the *prism* in its various form itions of planes, the *octahedron* or *decahedron* and *cosahedron*, or bodies with 8, 12 and 20 equal sides or faces etc , etc. However interesting and instructive this course may be we prefer to begin with somewhat simpler performances leaving this branch of this department for future time

The child receives a small quantity of clay, (wax may also be used,) a wooden knife, a small board, and a piece of oiled paper, on which it performs the work   If clay is used, this material should be kept in wet rags, in a cool place, and the object formed of it, dried in the sun, or in a mildly heated stove, and then coated with gum arabic, or varnish, which gives them the appearance of crockery

First, the child forms a sphere, from which it may produce many objects If it attaches a stem to it, it is a cherry , if it adds depressions and elevations, which represent the dried calyx, it will look like an apple , from it the pear, nut, potato, a head, may be molded, etc   Many small balls made to adhere to one another may produce a bunch of grapes, (Figs 1—5)

From the ball or sphere, a cylindrical body may be formed, by rolling on the board, usually called by the children a loaf of bread, cigar, a candle, loaf of sugar, etc

A bottle, a bag filled with flour or something else, can also easily be produced

Very soon the child will present the cube, an old acquaintance and playmate From it, it produces a house, a box a coffee mill and similar things Soon other forms of life will grow into existence, as plates dishes, animals and human beings houses, churches, birds' nests, etc etc If this occupation is intended to be more than mere entertainment, it is necessary to guide the activity of the child in a definite direction

The best direction to be followed in Froe-

bel's occupations is that for the development of regular forms of bodies Fundamental form, of course, is the sphere The child represents it easily, if perhaps not exactly true

By pressing and assisted by his knife, the one plane of the sphere is changed to several planes, corners, edges which produces the cube If the child changes its corners to planes (indicated in Fig 12,) a form of fourteen sides is produced If this process is continued so that the planes of the cube are changed to corners, the octahedron is the result, (Fig 13) By continued change of edges to planes and of planes to corners the most important regular forms of crystallization will be produced, which occupation, however, as mentioned before, belongs rather to a higher grade of school, and is therefore better postponed until after the Kinder-Garten training

Some regular bodies are more easily formed from the cylinder, the mediation between the sphere and cube By a pressure of the hand, or by means of his knife, the child changes the one round plane to three or four planes, and as many edges, producing thereby the prism and the four-sided column

If we change one of the planes of the cylinder to a corner, by forming a round plane from its center to the periphery of the plane we produce a cone If we change the surface of the cone to three or four planes, we shall have a three or four sided pyramid If we act in the same manner with the other end of the cylinder, we shall form a double cone, and from it we may produce a three or four-sided double pyramid, etc If we act in an opposite manner, destroy the edges of the cylinder, we shall again have the sphere

Well formed specimens may, to acquire greater durability, be treated as indicated previously The production of forms and figures from soft and pliable material belongs undoubtedly, to the earliest and most natural occupations of the human race, and has served all plastic arts as a starting point The occu

pation of modeling, then, is eminently fit to
carry into practice Froebel's idea that children, in their occupations, have to pass through
all the general grades of development of hu
man culture in a diminished scale The
natural talent of the future architect or sculp
tor, lying dormant in the child, must needs be
called forth and developed by this occupation,
as by a self acting and inventing construction
and formation, all innate talents of the child
are made to grow into visible reality

If we now cast a retrospective look upon
the means of occupation in the Kinder-
Garten, we find that the material progresses
form the *solid* and *whole*, in gradual steps to
its *parts*, until it arrives at the *image* upon
the *plane* and its conditions as to *line* and
point For the heavy material fit only to be
placed upon the table in unchanged form,
(the building blocks,) a more flexible one
is substituted in the following occupations
wood is replaced by *paper* The paper *plane*
of the folding occupation, is replaced by the
paper *strip* of the weaving occupation, as *line*
The wooden *staff*, or very thin *wire*, is then
introduced for the purpose of executing permanent figures in connection with *peas*, representing the *point* In place of this material
the *drawn line* then appears, to which *colors*
are added Perforating and embroidering
introduces another addition to the material
to create the images of fantasy, which, in the
paper cutting and mounting, again receive
new elements

The *modeling* in clay, or wax, affords the immediate plastic artistic occupation, with the
most pliable material for the hand of the
child *Song* introduces into the realm of
sound, when *movement plays, gymnastics,* and
dancing, help to educate the body, and insure
a harmonious development of all its parts
In practicing the technical manual perform
ances of the mechanic, such as boring,
piercing cutting, measuring uniting, forming
drawing painting, and modeling, a foundation
of all future occupation of artisan and artist

—synonymous in past centuries—is laid For
ornamentation especially, all elements are
found in the occupations of the Kinder Gar
ten The forms of beauty in the paper folding *f i*, serve as series of rosettes and ornaments in relief, as architecture might employ them, without change The productions
in the braiding department contain all conditions of artistic weaving, nor does the cut
ting of figures fail to afford richest material
for ornamentation of various kinds

For every talent in man means of develop
ment are provided in the Kinder Garten material, opportunity for practice is constantly
given, and each direction of the mind finds
its starting point in *concrete* things No more
complete satisfaction, therefore, can be given
to the claim of modern pedagogism, that all
ideas should be founded on previous percep
tion derived from real objects, than is done in
the genuine Kinder Garten

Whosoever has acquired even a superfi
cial idea only of the significance of Froebel's
means of occupation in the Kinder Garten,
will be ready to admit that the ordinary playthings of children can not, by any means, as
regards their usefulness, be compared with
the occupation material in the Kinder-Garten That the former may, in a certain de
gree be made helpful in the development of
children, is not denied , occasional good results with them, however, mostly always will
be found to be owing to the child's own in
stinct rather than to the nature of the toy
Planless playing, without guidance and supervision cannot prepare a child for the earnest
sides of life as well as for the enjoyment of
its harmless amusements and pleasures
Like the plant, which in the wilderness even,
draws from the soil its nutrition, so the child s
mind draws from its surroundings and the
means, placed at its command, its educational
food But the rose bush, nursed and cared
for in the garden by the skillful horticulturist
produces flowers, far more perfect and beautiful than the wild growing sweet briar Without care neither mind nor body of the child

can be expected to prosper   As the latter can not, for a healthful development, use all kinds of food without careful selection, so the mind for its higher cultivation requires a still more careful choice of the means for its development   The child's free choice is limited only in so far as it is necessary to limit the amount of occupation material in order to fit it for systematic application   The child will find instinctively all that is requisite for its mental growth, if the proper material only be presented, and a guiding mind indicate its most appropriate use in accordance with a certain *law*

Froebel's genius has admirably succeeded in inventing the proper material as well as in pointing out its most successful application to prepare the child for all situations in future life, for all branches of occupation in the useful pursuits of mankind

When the Kinder-Garten was first established by him, it was prohibited in its original form and its inventor driven from place to place in his fatherland on account of his liberal educational principles, to be carried out in the Kinder Garten   The keen eye of monarchial government officials quickly saw that such institution could not turn out willing subjects to tyrannical oppression, and the rulers *"by the grace of God,'* tolerated the Kinder Garten, only when public opinion declared too strongly in its favor

In pleading the cause of the Kinder Garten on the soil of republican America, is it asking too much that all may help in extending to the future generation the benefits which may be derived from an institution so eminently fit to educate free citizens of a free country ?

KINDER-GARTEN CULTURE.

THE fundamental principle of the Kinder-Garten system of education, so clearly laid down in his writings, and so successfully carried out in practice by Friedrich Froebel, is expressed in the axiom, that, before ideas can be defined, perceptions must have preceded, objects must have been presented to the senses, and by their examination experiences acquired of their being, quality and action, of which definite ideas are the logical results, with which they are therefore inseparably connected. It is not claimed that this principle originated with the inventor of the Kinder Garten, for long before him it was said that 'Nihil est in intellectu, quod antea non fuerit in sensu," but, in the Kinder-Garten system, he has furnished all material to begin the education of mankind on this logical basis.

Definite ideas are to originate as abstractions from perceptions (*Anschauungen,* as the Germans say, meaning literally *the looking at,* or *into things*) If they do not originate in such manner they are not the product of one's own mental activity, but simply the consent of the understanding to the ideas of others. By far the greatest part of all acquired knowledge with the mass of the people, is of this kind. Every one, however, even the least gifted, may acquire a stock of fundamental perceptions, which shall serve as points of relation in the process of thinking. Indefinite or confused fundamental or elementary perceptions prevent understanding words with precision, which is necessary to reflecting on the ideas and thoughts of others with clearness, and appropriating them to one's self. In the fact that a large majority of persons are lacking in clear and distinct fundamental perceptions, we find cause for the existence of so many confused heads, full of the most absurd notions. The period of life in which the first fundamental perceptions are formed must necessarily be our earliest childhood. They can form only during this state of as it were, mental unconsciousness, because the impressions on the senses can best be fixed lastingly upon the soul, when this process is least disturbed by reflection, and impressions of objects of the world without upon our senses, are made more or less clearly and distinctly, according to the nature of these objects themselves. A mere acquisition of perceptions, however, is not sufficient

As in the development of all organism in nature, a certain, peculiar series of events takes place, which always must be the same, or at least take place in accordance with the same law, to reach the same aim, or produce the same form, so, also, in mental development, a peculiar process, a natural series of events must take place without disturbing occurrences, to successfully reach the corresponding idea in the mind. This series of events in the mind and heart, connected with the process of thinking, is in philosophy explained to consist of   1st A general or total impression   2d A perception or looking on a single thing   3d Observation of qualities and relations   4th Comparison   5th Judging   6th Conclusion   Although a right selection of objects, and their proper succession, are of the first importance, adherence to these two conditions is not yet sufficient to prepare and accustom the mind to logical thinking, these means should be applied or presented in a systematic, methodical way, also   A system of education in perfect accordance with the laws of nature is only possible, therefore, when the *modus operandi* of the natural functions of the soul, during their development is fully understood, and the exact means are discovered to assist these functions in a corresponding manner from without   As long as this is not done, the education of the human race is left to be the result of chance, and at the mercy of mere educational instinct   We claim that the significance of Froebel's educational system consists mainly in a perfect understanding of the natural process of mental development   This understanding guided him in preparing certain means of education, or play, all following the same course as the mental development which they are intended to promote   No man has ever looked so deeply as Friedrich Froebel into the secret workshop of a child's soul, and so successfully discovered the means and their methodical application for a development of the young mind in accordance with nature's own laws   To be certain that the natural course of development be not interrupted but logically assisted, the child's instinct should have free choice within appointed limits, and still be obliged to receive the objects as they are presented to it for the first perceptions. The means to obtain this, Froebel has found in allowing the child to manipulate the things destined for the production of changes according to his own choice Thereby the child will be led to devote attention to the objects formed, because he looks upon them as his own work, and rejoices in what he is able *to do* That free unrestricted activity of the child, which we call play, alone can comply with these conditions, anything else *forced* upon the child, can never be successfully employed for this purpose A desire of acquiring knowledge of things, is an innate faculty of the soul, hence there is no need of *forcing* the child into making acquaintance with the things given him to play with We have only to select for his playthings the fundamental forms, which, like the typical formations in nature, offer, as it were, a fundamental scheme for an acquaintance with the large multitude of things Knowledge of things can be acquired only by acquisition of a knowledge of their qualities We then have to provide objects in which the general qualities of things are shown in perfect distinctness, in order to produce thereby clear and lasting perceptions in the mind of the child These objects should be such that they may be easily manipulated by the limited strength of the child, that he may become acquainted with them by their use, and become enabled thereby to gather experiences in regard to events and facts in the physical world, and may, so to say, serve him for the first physical experiments Examining the list of Froebel's Kinder-Garten occupation material, we find it to consist of the following

1 Six soft balls of various colors
2 Sphere, cube, and cylinder, made of wood
3 Large cube, divided into eight small cubes
4 Large cube, divided into eight oblong blocks
5 Large cube, consisting of 21 whole, 6 half and 12 quarter cubes
6 Large cube, consisting of 18 whole oblongs with 3 divided lengthwise and 6 divided breadthwise
7 Quadrangular, and various triangular tablets for laying figures
8 Staffs or wands for laying figures
9 Whole and half wire rings for laying figures
10 Material for drawing
11 Material for perforating
12 Material for embroidering
13 Material for paper cutting and combining the parts into symmetrical figures
14 Material for weaving or braiding
15 Slats for interlacing

16 Slats with 4, 6, 8, and 16 links
17 Paper strips for lacing
18. Material for paper folding
19 Material for peas work
20 Material for modeling *

The list begins with the *ball*, an object, comprising in itself, in the simplest manner, the general qualities of all things As the starting point of form—the spherical—it gives the first impression of form, and being the most easily moved of all forms, is symbolical of life It becomes the first known object, with which all other objects for the child's play are brought into relation Beside teaching form, the balls are also intended to teach *color*, hence their number of six, representing three primary and three secondary colors The principle of combining, uniting, or bringing into relation of *opposites*, which is a governing law throughout all occupations in the Kinder Garten, is applied here to discriminating primary and secondary colors, the latter being produced by a combination of two of the former †

For the purpose of acquiring clear and distinct, correct ideas of things around us, it is indispensably necessary to become acquainted with them in all respects and relations The balls are made the object of a great variety of plays or occupations, to make the child become well acquainted with its uses, and to enable him to handle it gracefully Then, for the purpose of comparison, the second Gift is introduced, consisting of *sphere, cube,* and *cylinder* We can here, certainly not yet speak of a rational comparison on the part of the young child, but simply of an immediate, sensual perception or observation of the similarities and differences existing in the things presented The child will find by looking at the three new objects exhibited to him that the sphere is just like the ball, except in its material The first impression, that of roundness, made upon the child by the many colored, soft balls, finds here its further development by the fact that this quality is found in this wooden ball, or *the sphere*, as he may be led to name it, learning a new word To facilitate the process of comparison, the objects to be compared should first be as different as possible, *opposites* in a certain sense The opposition between sphere and cube relates to their form Together with the oppositional, or difference in objects, their similarity should in the meantime be made prominent, for comparison demands to detect equality and similarity of things as well as their

---

* The above arrangement and numbering of the Gifts adopted by writers on the Kinder Garten and manufacturers of its occupation material, has been retained here, as a change could not well be made without producing much confusion The logical connection of the Gifts, as described in this paper, can not be affected in the least by the numbers attached to them for the purpose of designating them as articles of manufacture

† When the secondary colors are presented, it would be well to have three pieces of glass of the three primary colors, and let the children take two and look through them toward the light which would teach them sensuously the combinations.

distinction by inequality and dissimilarity. The cylinder introduced as the mediatory between the opposites in form, given here, is the simplest and immediately suggested mediative form, because it combines the qualities of both *cube* and *sphere* in itself.

These three *whole* bodies, introduced as fundamental or normal forms or shapes, in which all qualities of whole bodies in general are demonstrated, and which serve to convey the idea of an impression of the *whole*, are followed by the introduction of *variously divided* solid bodies. Without a division of the whole, observation and recognition, *i e*, knowledge of it, is next to impossible. The rational investigation, the dissecting and dividing by the mind, in short, *the analysis* should be preceded by a like process in real objects, if the mind is calculated to reflect upon nature. Division performed at random, however, can never give clear ideas of the whole or its parts, but a regular division, in accordance with certain laws, is always needed. Nature gives us also here the best instruction. She performs all her divisions according to mathematical laws.

The orders in the vegetable kingdom are distinguished according to form and number of parts. Froebel here, also, borrowed from nature a guide which led him in systematizing the means of development of the young mind in the Kinder Garten.

As the first *divided* body, a large cube is introduced, consisting of eight small cubes of the same size each, as its parts. The large cube is divided once in each direction of space, lengthwise, breadthwise and hightwise. The form of the *parts* is here like the form of the *whole*, and only their relation as to volume is different. In shape, alike, they differ in size, which fact becomes more apparent by a variety of combinations of a different number of the parts. Thus the relation of number is here introduced to the observation of the child, together with that of form and magnitude. A clear and distinct idea of these relations could hardly be attained unless presented in this manner. In the following Gift, diversity of form in the whole and its parts, is made apparent, preceding the introduction of the relations of the plane. The logical connection with the preceding Gifts consists in the same form of the whole, the cube, and the same manner of division; the 5th and 6th being divided twice, whereas the 3d and 4th were divided only once in all directions of space. The variety of forms gained, by this division of the cube, give the widest scope to the invention and production of combined forms, without ever leading to an indefinite, unlimited, unrestrained activity. The logical combination of parts to a whole which is required in using these blocks, renders it a preparatory occupation for succeeding combinations of thought, for, also the

construction of parts into a whole follows certain laws, thereby forming a serial connection, which, in nature, is represented by the membering or linking of all organisms. As nature, in the organic world, begins to form by agglomeration, so the child in its first occupations commences with mere accumulation of parts. Order, however, is requisite to lead to the beautiful in the visible world, as logic is indispensable in the world of thought for the formation of clear ideas, and Froebel's law *to link opposites*, affords the simplest and most reliable guide to this end.

In the building occupation this law, f 1, is applied in relation to the joining of blocks according to their *form*, or the different position of the parts in relation to a common center. If I join sides and sides, or edges and edges of the blocks, I have formed *opposites*; side and edge or edge and side joined, are considered as links or mediation. Thus below and above are opposites in relation to which the right and left side of form or figure built, serve as mediative parts. Carrying out this principle, we have established a most admirable order, by which even the youngest pupil, frequently unknowingly, produces the most charming regular forms and figures. This regular and serial constructing of the *parts* to a *whole*, according to a determinate law, is followed by connecting various wholes with one another, to produce orders and series as we find them in all the natural kingdoms, just as we are in need of categories in the process of thinking. Therefore we produce in the Kinder Garten, by means of our occupation material, *different series* of forms and figures from common *elementary forms*, which we call either *forms of life, forms of knowledge*, or *forms of beauty*. The first are representations of objects actually existing and coming under our common observation, as the works of human skill and art.

The second are such as afford instruction relative to *number, order proportion*, etc. The third are figures representing only *ideal* forms, yet so regularly constructed as to present perfect models of symmetry and order in arrangement of parts. By occupation with these differently, yet always regularly constructed bodies, the child will make observations of the greatest variety, which, by immediate use of the objects by manipulation and experiment, make a real experience. The observations f 1 of the vertical and horizontal, of the right angled, of the directions of up and downward, of under, above and next one another, of regularity, of equipoise, the relation of circumference and center, of multiplication and division, of all that produces harmony in construction, etc, impress themselves, as it were, indelibly upon the child's mind almost at every step. The first knowledge, or rather idea of the qualities of matter, and the first experiences of its use, are obtained thus in the simplest manner and delightfully Thus the lawful shaping, logical development and methodical application of the material, is, as it were, the logic of nature imitated, whose representation is found in the forms of crystallization It is natural that the works of God should reflect the logic of the great Creator's mind, and thereby be made the teachers of mankind What can man do better in educating the human mind, than imitate these means, for the purpose of unfolding and strengthening the germ of logic, implanted in the mind of every human being, created in the image of his God

A condition of indisputable importance for the acquisition of knowledge of things, is the knowledge of the material of which they consist, and their qualities, and this should be introduced in right succession From the 2d to the 6th Gifts, the objects consist of *wood*, and they are in the meantime solid bodies

The next step in the use of matter as the representation of mind, is the transition to the plane, Froebel's Tablets for laying figures In them, the simple mathematic fundamental forms are given as embodied planes, beginning with the square, which is followed successively by the right angled triangle with two equal sides, (1-2 square,) the right angled triangle with unequal sides, the obtuse-angled triangle, and the equilateral triangle

The *slats* given for the play of interlacing form the transition from the *plane* to the *line*, resembling the latter, although, owing to their width, still occupying space as a plane They represent in one respect a progress beyond the staffs, because they may be joined for the purpose of representing lasting forms

The *staffs*, representing the embodied line, facilitate the elements of drawing, serving as movable outlines of planes They are to be looked upon as the divided plane in order to adhere to their connections and relation with the form from which we started By means of the staffs, numerical relation first is made more prominent and evident by the introduction of figures The application of the law of opposites relates in all previous occupations to the *form* and *direction* of parts

In the so-called *peas work* the staffs (eventually wire) are united by *points*, represented by peas, demonstrating that it is union which produces lasting formation of matter

Here closes the first section of Froebel's embodied alphabet, intended to give the elemental images for the succeeding recognition of complex form, magnitude and numerical relations Thus the child has been guided in a logical manner from the *solid body* through its *divisions* and through the embodied plane, line and point, in matter and by matter, to the borders of the abstract, without going over into abstraction, which is a later process, to be postponed to the

school that succeeds to the Kinder Garten To *reduce* or "*lead back*" mathematical perception (abstract thinking) to appearances in the material world, no more appropriate means and method could have been devised All abstractions are drawn—*abstracted* according to the original meaning of the word—from manifestations of the visible world Although further final conclusions (which may be continued ad infinitum) shall remove them from their origin, elevate them to the loftiest hights of thought, their roots are ever to be looked for in the material world The assertion that ideas are founded and defined by perceptions only, is either entirely erroneous and not to be proved, or there must exist such a connection, such an analogy, between the things of the material world and the objects of thought, as has been indicated here And if it can be proved that such a course of development of the human mind necessarily takes place in some degree without our assistance, as a natural process, then education should not dare to prescribe any other one ; then this is the only true method of developing the mind, because it operates with nature's laws, although it does not exclude all assistance on our part, but invokes it We have often opportunity to notice how easily the mind, without human assistance, grows in *wrong* directions, like the young tree that never felt the effect of the pruning knife

In the following occupations of the Kinder Garten we shall notice the progress from the solid *body* or *object itself* to the representation of its *image* by drawing Planes and lines, the various forms of the triangle and other geometric figures, occur also here, but they are produced by different material The touching or handling of the solid body, the most important means of acquiring knowledge during the first years of a child's life, during the state of its rational unconsciousness, is now entirely changed to a looking at objects presented to its observation ; and the image of the body, so to say, takes the place of the body itself Drawing with pencil is of such paramount importance because the child is enabled by it to reproduce quickly and easily the images imparted to its mind by their own visible representation, whereby they become truly objective and are only then fully understood Instruction in writing should never precede instruction in drawing

In the development of the human race, the body unmistakably precedes its image or representation, as the drawn image preceded the written sign or letter In the incipient stages of civilization, these signs for things were images, as we see in all hieroglyphic inscriptions Our modern letters occupy the highest step in the scale of the language of signs (which we should not forget)

Froebel's method of instruction in drawing is as

ingenious as it is simple The same course as pursued in the study of things, according to their form,
size and number, and mathematical proportions is
also here adhered to The various forms which have
previously occupied the child in their existence as
bodies, appear here in drawn pictures, and are multiplied ad infinitum The progression from the simplest rudiment to the more complicated, the great
multiplicity of series, determined by the various directions of the lines and the geometric fundamental forms
the logical progression from the straight to the curved
lines, render drawing—not considering here its immediate artistic significance — one of the most ef-
ficient means for disciplining the mind of the young
pupil It is the first step for the child to a future
careful observation of the general connection of things
from the smallest to the largest, as parts as well as
wholes

In the following occupations, the material of which
is a more refined one, color is introduced in connection with multiplication of form, and the products of
the children's work are constantly approaching real
artistic creations In the *braiding* or *weaving* the
thought of *number* is predominating because the opposites of odd and even are combined by alternately
employing both In the *paper-folding*, opposites are
formed by the oppositional directions of the lines,
(horizontal or perpendicular) originating in the folding
of the paper, and these opposites are connected by
the mediative oblique line In like manner this law
is applied to angles, acute and obtuse as opposites,
the right angle serving as a mediatory This is repeated in the occupation of *perforating* and *embroidering* The *cutting of paper*, also, especially affords a
perfect view of all the mathematical elements for the
purpose of plastic representation

Thus we find everywhere the same logical chain of
perception, and subsequent representation and exper-
imental knowledge resulting from both, and thus all
parts and sections of this system of occupation are
logically united with one another, serving the child's
mind as a faithful reflector of its own internal development at each and every step And well may the
matured mind, developed according to these principles, in future days retrace with facility its concerning
and thinking to the clear and sharply defined, as it
were, typical images of this reflector, as their very
origin, for such experiences surely can never be ef-
faced

It has been charged by those who have only a superficial knowledge of Froebel's educational system,
that by it the faculties of the young mind are too
soon awakened, which should not be taxed at so
early an age To this accusation we invite the most
careful investigation, the result of which, we doubt

not, will be a conviction that just the opposite is the
case

Manual occupation, performed in connection with
all means of occupation in the Kinder Garten, con-
tinual representation of objects, plastic formation and
production, are all attractive to the nature of the child
and touch the springs of spontaneity in its very core
All observations which appeal to the understanding
and prepare mathematical conceptions occur, as it
were, as accessories only, and to such an extent as the
child's desire calls for them Nothing is ever *forced*
upon the pupil's mind It can not even be said that
teaching is prominent, but rather practical occupation,
individually intended production, on the part of the
children, which give rise to most of the remarks required to be made on the part of the Kinder Gartner
The element of *working*, which every child's nature
craves, is predominating Activity of the hand is the
fundamental condition of all development in the child,
as it is also the fundamental condition for the acquisition of *knowledge*, and the subjection of matter Mechanical ability, technical dexterity, education of all
human senses require under all circumstances manual
occupation However, if this side of Froebel's educational system is mentioned, another class of op-
ponents is ready to object, that the child should not
begin with work, but that first its mind should be developed We understand these various objections to
mean that the child's powers should not be employed
in mechanical occupation exclusively, nor be entirely
deprived of it, but that a harmonious development of
body and mind should be the task of education This
is in perfect accordance with Froebel's principles,
which, if carried out rightly, will accomplish this in
the fullest meaning of the word No occupation in
the Kinder Garten is merely mechanical, it is one of
the most important rules that the mere mechanical,
as contrary to the child's nature, should studiously be
avoided

Nothing is plainer to the careful observer of the
child's nature than the desire of the little mind to observe and imbibe *all* its surroundings with *all* its senses
simultaneously It wishes to see, to hear, to feel, all
beautiful, joyful, and pleasant things and then strives
to reproduce them as *far* as its limited faculties will
admit To receive and give back, is life, life in all its
directions, with all its powers This is what the child
desires, what it should be led to accomplish with a
view to its own development Eyes and ears seek
the beautiful, the senses of taste and smell enjoy the
agreeable, and the impression which this beautiful and
agreeable make upon the child's mind calls forth in
the child's innermost soul, the desire, nay, the necessity of production, representation, or formation If
we should neglect providing the means to gratify such

desire, a full development of the heart of the individual, a higher taste for the ideal in it, never could be
the result We believe that this desire can not be
assisted more perfectly and appropriately than by ac-
complishment in *form, color,* and *tone,* each expressing and representing in its own manner, the feeling of
the beautiful and agreeable The earlier such accom-
plishment is begun, the more perfectly the heart or
æsthetic sentiment in man will be developed, the more
surely a foundation for the moral development of the
individual be laid   Aptness in formation and produc
tion conditions development of the hand, simultaneously with the development of the senses It conditions, also, knowledge and subjection of matter and
the proper material for the yet weak and unskilled
hand of children Formation itself furthermore conditions observation of the various relations of form,
size, and number, as shown in connection with the
gifts, employed for the preparatory development of
the perceptive faculties Mathematical forms and figures are, as it were, the skeleton of the beautiful in
form, which, in its perfection always requires the
curved line Images of ancient peoples, as we find
them f 1 in the Egyptian temples are straight lined,
hence are geometrical figures The curved line, the
true line of beauty, we find subsequently, when the
artistic feeling had become more fully developed
The forms of *beauty* alternating in all branches of Kin
der-Garten occupation, with those of life and knowledge, afford the most appropriate means for the development of a sense of art as well as of aptness in
art, in the meantime preventing a one sided prevalence
of a mere cold understanding

The faculties of the soul are not yet distinctly sep
arated in the young child the understanding, feeling
and will, act in union with one another and every one
is developed through and with the others The com
binations of the power of representation in formation
serve also as the preliminary exercise for that combination of thought, and what the hand produces
strengthens the will and energy of the young mind in
the meantime affording gratification to the heart All
work of man, be it common manual work, or a work
of art, or purely mental labor is always the uniting of
parts to a whole, i e , *organizing* in the highest sense
of the word The more we are conscious of aim,
means, manner and method connected with our work,
the more the mind is active in it, the higher and no-
bler the result will be The lowest step of human
labor is formed by mechanical imitation, the highest is
free formation or production, according to one's own
conception Between these two points we find the
whole scale by which the crudest kind of labor mounts
to a free production in art and science and on which
invention stands uppermost as the gradual triumphant

result from simplest imitation It is this scale *en min
nature* through which the child's mind is conducted by
means of Froebel's occupation material From the
first immediate impression, received from objects and
forms of the visible world, it rises *to art,* or creation
according to own ideas, which is its own production,
a self-willed formation For this purpose nature implanted in the human mind a strong desire to produce
form, which, if correctly guided, becomes the most
useful faculty of the soul Simply by this desire of
formation the images of perception attain the neces
sary perfect distinctness and clearness, the power of
observation, its keenness and experience, its proofs,
all of which are requisite, to afford to the working of the
human mind a sure foundation Free invention, creat
ing, is the culminating point of mental independence
We lead the child to this eminence by degrees Some
times accident has led to invention and production of
the new, but Froebel has provided a systematically
graded method by which infancy may at once start
upon the road to this eminent aim of inventing

If the full consciousness, the clear conception of its
aim is at first wanting, it is prepared by every step
onward The objects presented, and the material em
ployed, afford the child, under the guidance of a ma
ture mind, the alphabet of art, as well as that of
knowledge, and it is worth while here to remark that
history shows art comes before science in all human
development

If we now cast a retrospective glance upon the
means of occupation in the Kinder Garten, we find
that the material progresses from the *solid* and *whole* in
gradual steps to its *parts,* until it arrives at the *image*
upon the *plane* and its conditions as to *line* and *point*
For the heavy material, fit only to be placed upon the
table in unchanged form (the building blocks), a more
flexible one is substituted in the following occupations
Wood is replaced by *paper* The paper plane of the
folding occupation, is replaced by the paper *strip* of
the weaving occupation, as *line* The wooden *staff*
or very fine *wire* is then introduced for the purpose of
executing permanent figures in connection with *peas,*
representing the *point* In place of this material the
drawn line then appears, to which *colors* are added
Perforating and embroidering introduces another ad
dition to the material to create the images of fantasy
which, in the paper cutting and mounting, again re
ceive new elements The modeling in clay or wax
affords the immediate plastic artistic occupation, with
the most pliable material for the hand of the child
Song introduces into the realm of sound, when *move
ment plays, gymnastics* and *dancing* help to educate the
body and insure a harmonious development of all its
parts In practicing the technical manual perform
ances of the mechanic, such as boring, piercing, cut

ting, measuring, uniting, forming, drawing, painting, and modeling, a foundation of all future occupation of artisan and artist—synonymous in classic and mediæval antiquity—is laid. For ornamentation, especially, all elements are found in the occupations of the Kinder Garten. The forms of beauty in the paper folding f i, serve as series of rosettes and ornaments in relief that architecture might employ without change. The productions in the braiding department contain all conditions of artistic weaving, nor does the cutting of figures fail to afford richest material for ornamentation of various kinds. For every talent in man means of development are provided in the Kinder Garten material. Opportunity for practice is constantly given, and each direction of the mind finds its starting-point in *concrete* things. No more complete satisfaction, therefore, can be given to the claim of rational education "that all ideas should be founded on previous perception, derived from real objects," than is done in the genuine Kinder Garten. Whosoever has acquired even a superficial idea only of the significance of Froebel's means of occupation in the Kinder Garten, will be ready to admit that the ordinary play things of children are not, by any means, as regards their usefulness, to be compared with the occupation material in the Kinder Garten. That the former in a certain degree, may be made helpful in the development of children, is not denied. Occasional good results with them, which, however, usually will be found to be owing to the child's own instinct rather than to the nature of the toy. Planless playing, without guidance and supervision, can not prepare a child for the earnest sides of life, or even for the enjoyment of its own harmless amusements and pleasures. Like the plant, which, even in the wilderness, draws from the soil its nutrition, so the child's mind draws from its surroundings and the means, placed at its command, its educational food. But the rose bush, nursed and cared for in the garden by the skillful horticulturist, produces flowers far more perfect and beautiful than the wild growing sweet briar. Without care neither the mind nor the body of the child can be expected to prosper. As the latter can not, for a healthful development, use all kinds of food without careful selection, so the mind for its higher cultivation requires a still more careful choice of the means for its development. The child's free choice is limited only in so far as it is necessary to limit the amount of occupation material in order to fit it for systematic application. The child will find, instinctively, all that is requisite for its mental growth, if the proper material only be presented, and a guiding mind indicate its most appropriate use in accordance with a certain *law*.

Froebel's genius has admirably succeeded in inventing the proper material as well as in pointing out its most successful application, to prepare the child for all situations in future life, for all branches of occupation in the useful pursuits of mankind. When the Kinder-Garten was first established by Froebel, it was prohibited, and its inventor driven from place to place in his fatherland on account of his liberal educational principles to be carried out in the Kinder Garten. The keen eye of monarchial government officials quickly saw that such institution would not turn out passive subjects to tyrannical oppression and the rulers *"by the grace of God"* tolerated the Kinder Garten only when public opinion declared too strongly in its favor to be safely resisted. In pleading the cause of the Kinder Garten on the soil of republican America, do I ask too much if I invite all to assist in extending to future generations the benefits to be derived from an institution so eminently fit to educate *free* citizens of a *free* country?

APPENDIX TO CHAPTER ON PERFORATING AND EMBROIDERY.

(Page 55)

Since the publication of the foregoing pages a considerable advance has been made in the occupation of embroidery, and the publishers take the liberty to make a few statements which they believe to be accepted facts, but for which the author of the book is in no way responsible.

Owing to the tax on the eyes, the perforating occupation has been deemed by many as rather undesirable if carried to any considerable extent, and hence it is not thought wise to require the child to perforate the elementary patterns for embroidery But this work, if thrown upon the teacher, would be too heavy a task and a useless waste of energy, as the patterns can be so much more rapidly pricked by machinery

Therefore Bradley's Pricked Cards were devised many years ago, the designs for which were based on the German school of embroidery More recently American Kindergartners have materially abridged the number of designs to be used in the course, and several years ago the ladies of the Florence Kindergarten made the selection illustrated in Plate La, which was styled the Florence School of Sewing This course has given good satisfaction to a large number of Kindergartners who have adopted it But as every thoughtful Kindergartner has her own ideas, suggestions for changes have been made from time to time, and a new arrangement illustrated in Plate Lb is the result of the conference of several experienced Kindergartners, and is christened the Winona School of Sewing

After vertical and horizontal lines, their combination into right angles, squares and oblongs follows, and the oblique line is not introduced even indirectly until the seventh card.

The diagonals of squares, singly and combined, follow in the next six cards, and the diagonals of vertical and horizontal oblongs, combined in the same order, fill the next twelve, some new designs having been made to complete the series

The rhombus follows naturally the diagonals of oblongs

This course gives children who are sufficiently advanced an opportunity to invent, which can be easily done on cards pricked regularly in squares

The entire series of cards comprises more than fifty different patterns of sewing, although in several instances the same pattern of pricking serves for more than one pattern of sewing There are also cards pricked in regular squares over the entire surface except a margin All the pattern cards are on white cardboard, the contrasts being secured in the colors of the worsteds, but the regularly perforated are in tints as well as white The pattern cards are $3\frac{3}{4}$x$4\frac{1}{2}$ inches The others in several sizes

Cards with outlines of natural objects for embroidery have long been in use, and are considered very desirable. A series of original designs is now offered, embracing animals, flowers, figures of children, and Christmas and New Year's cards

A complete illustrated list of all the above cards sent to any address on application to the publishers of this book

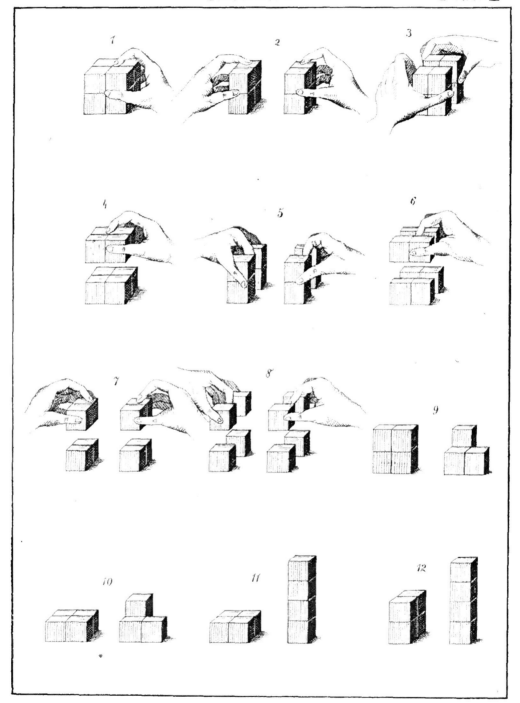

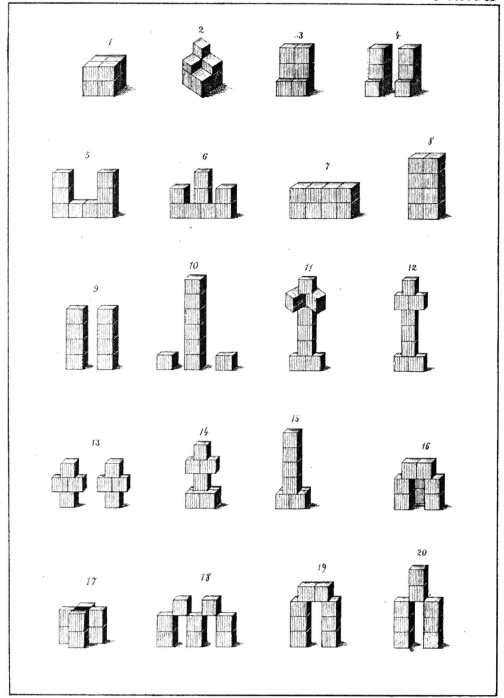

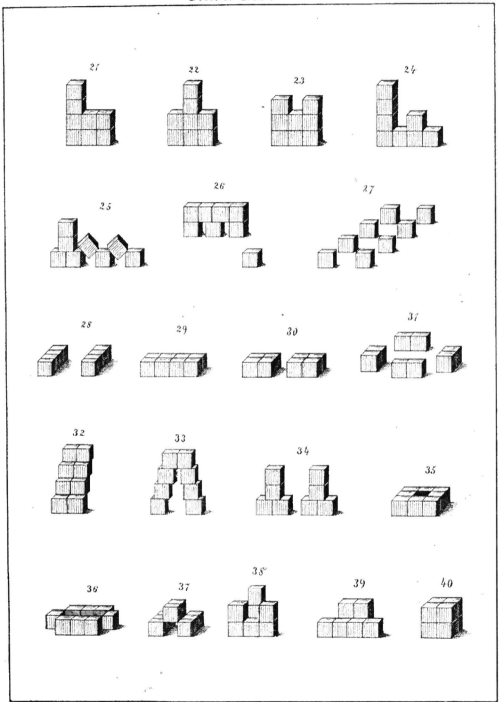

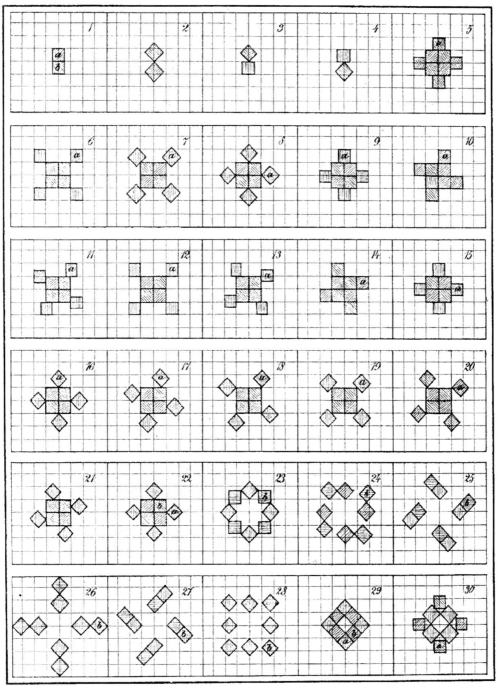

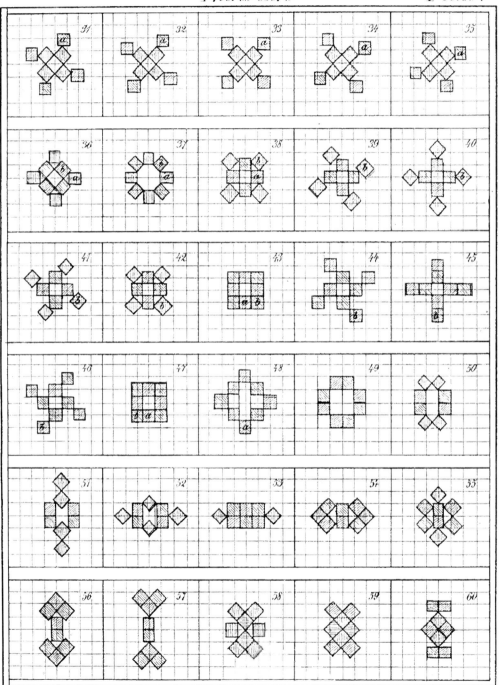

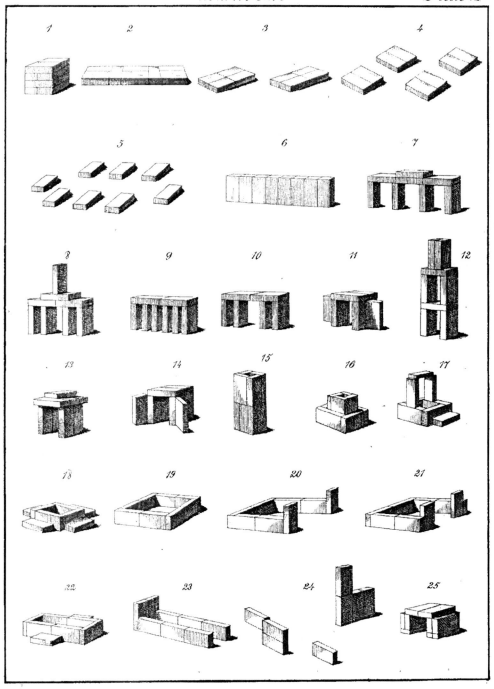

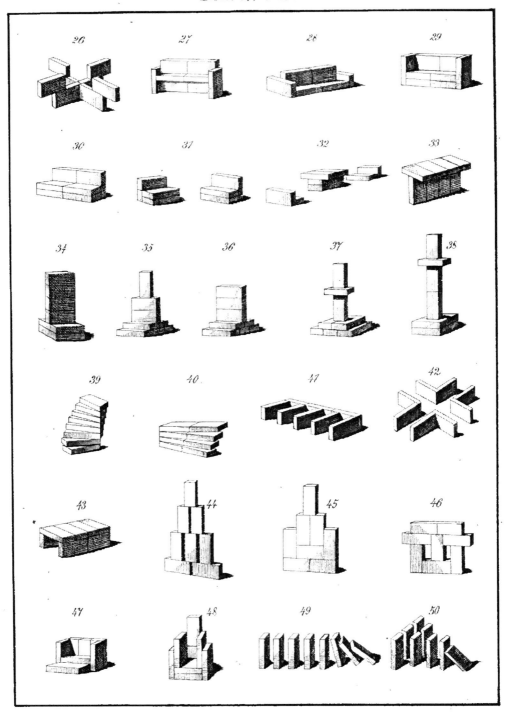

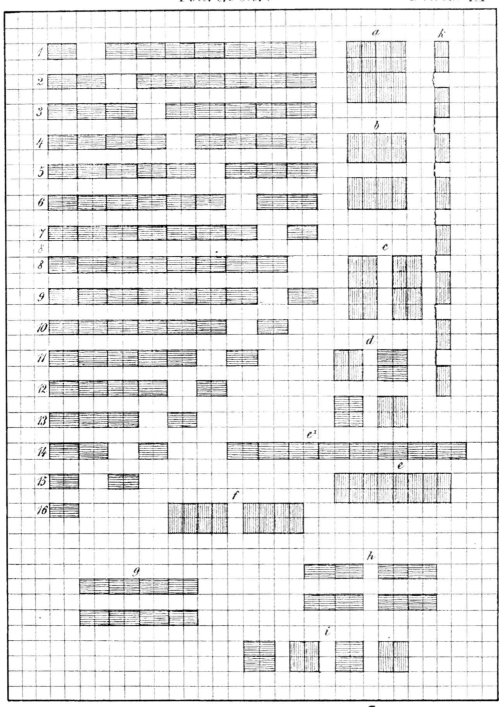

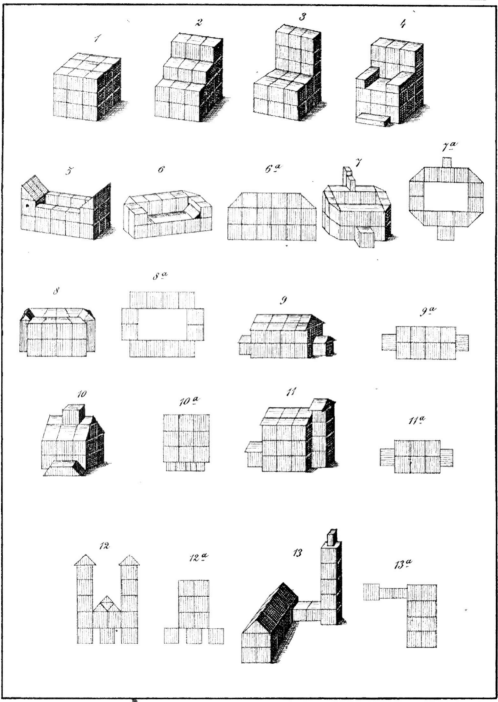

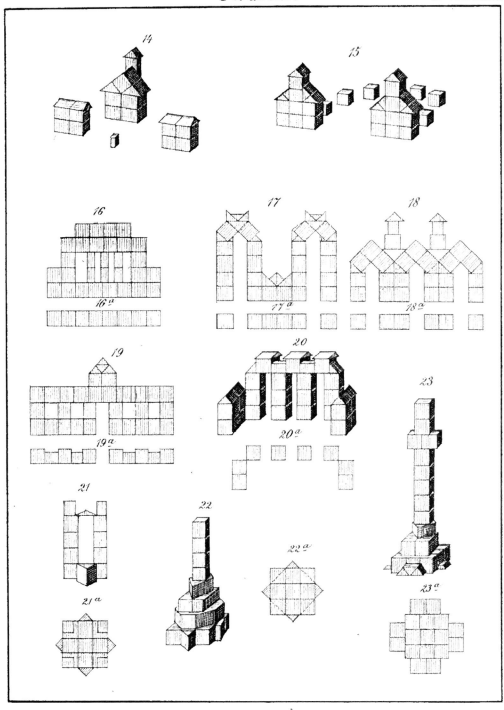

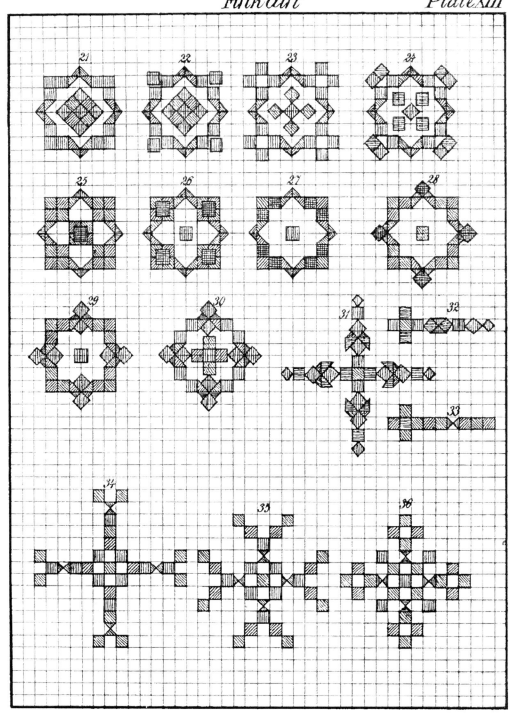

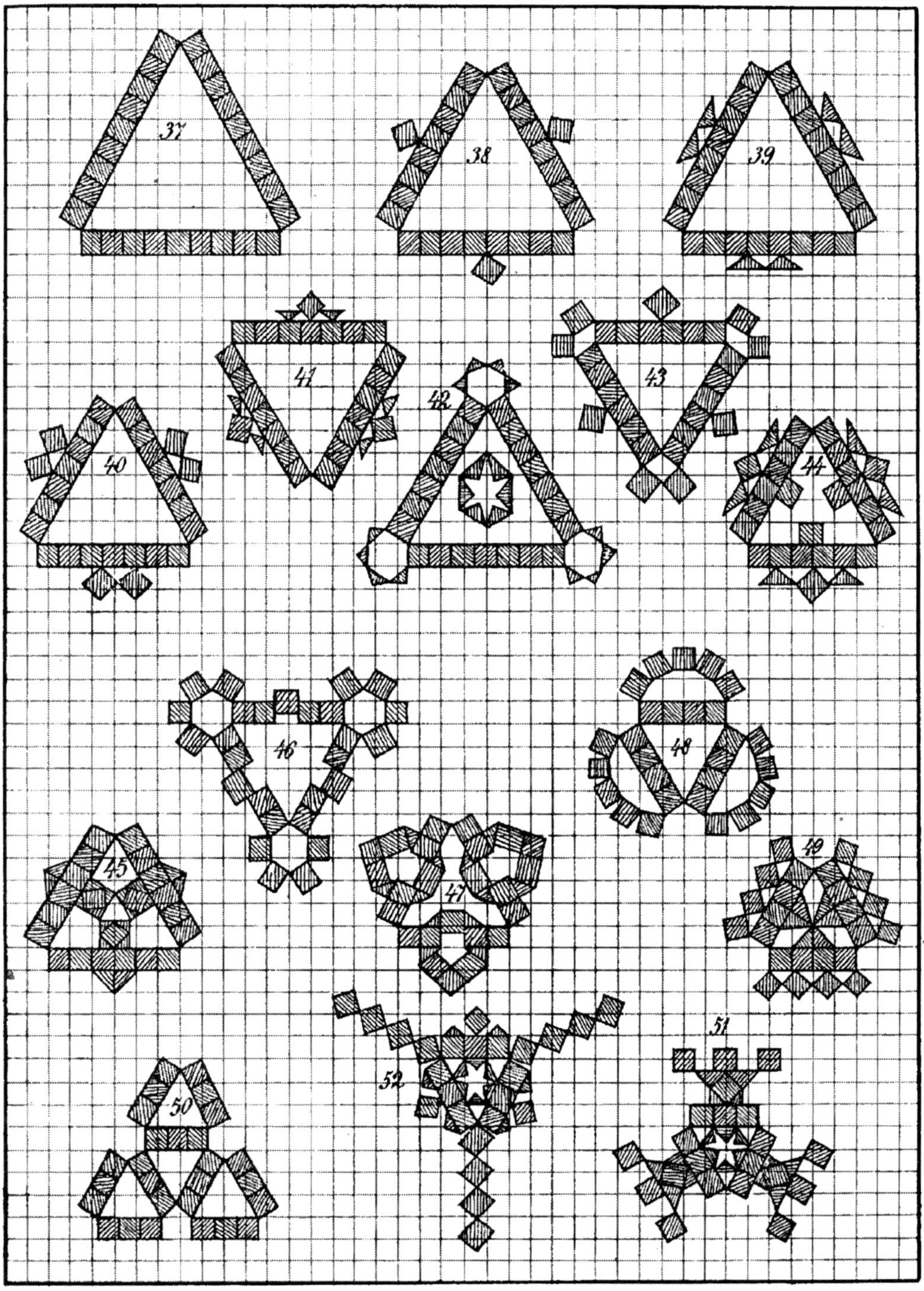
37
38
39
41
42
43
40
44
46
48
45
47
49
52
51
50

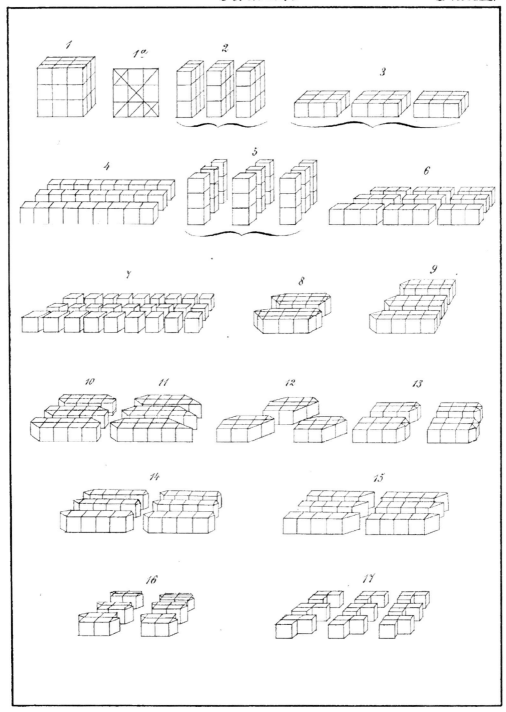

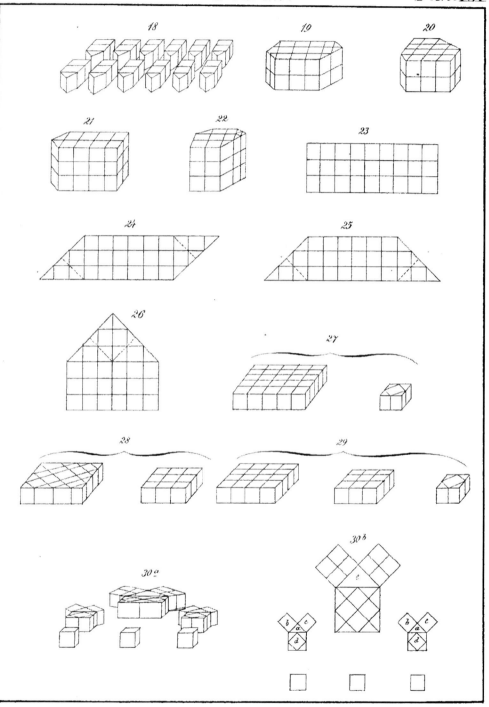

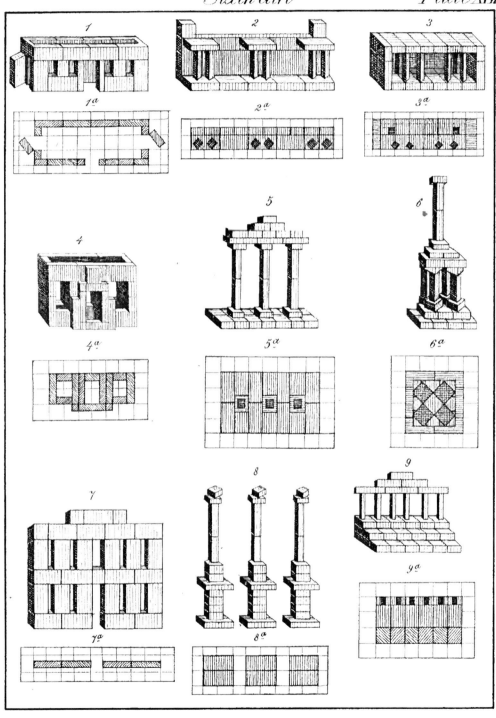

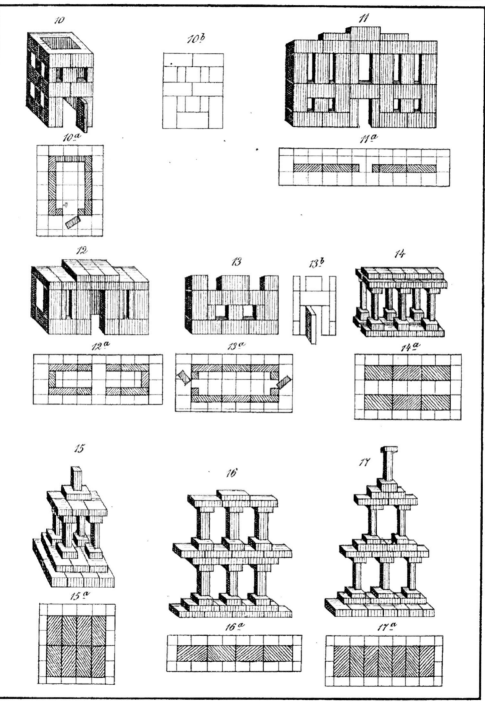

10

10ᵇ

11

10ᵃ

11ᵃ

12

13

13ᵇ

14

12ᵃ

13ᵃ

14ᵃ

15

16

17

15ᵃ

16ᵃ

17ᵃ

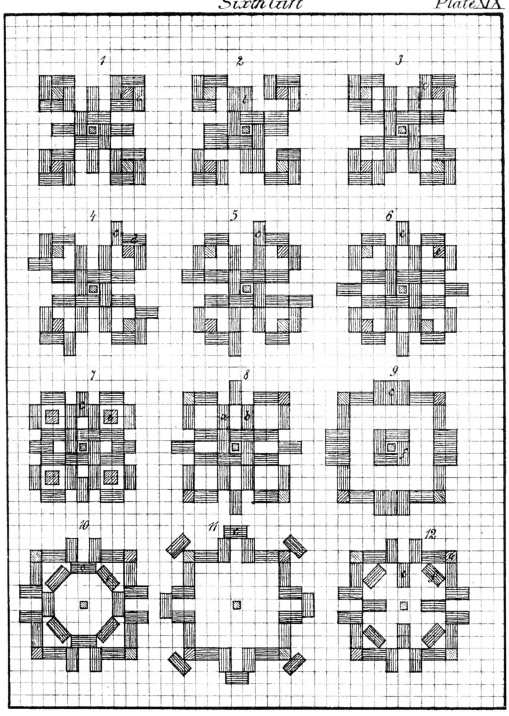

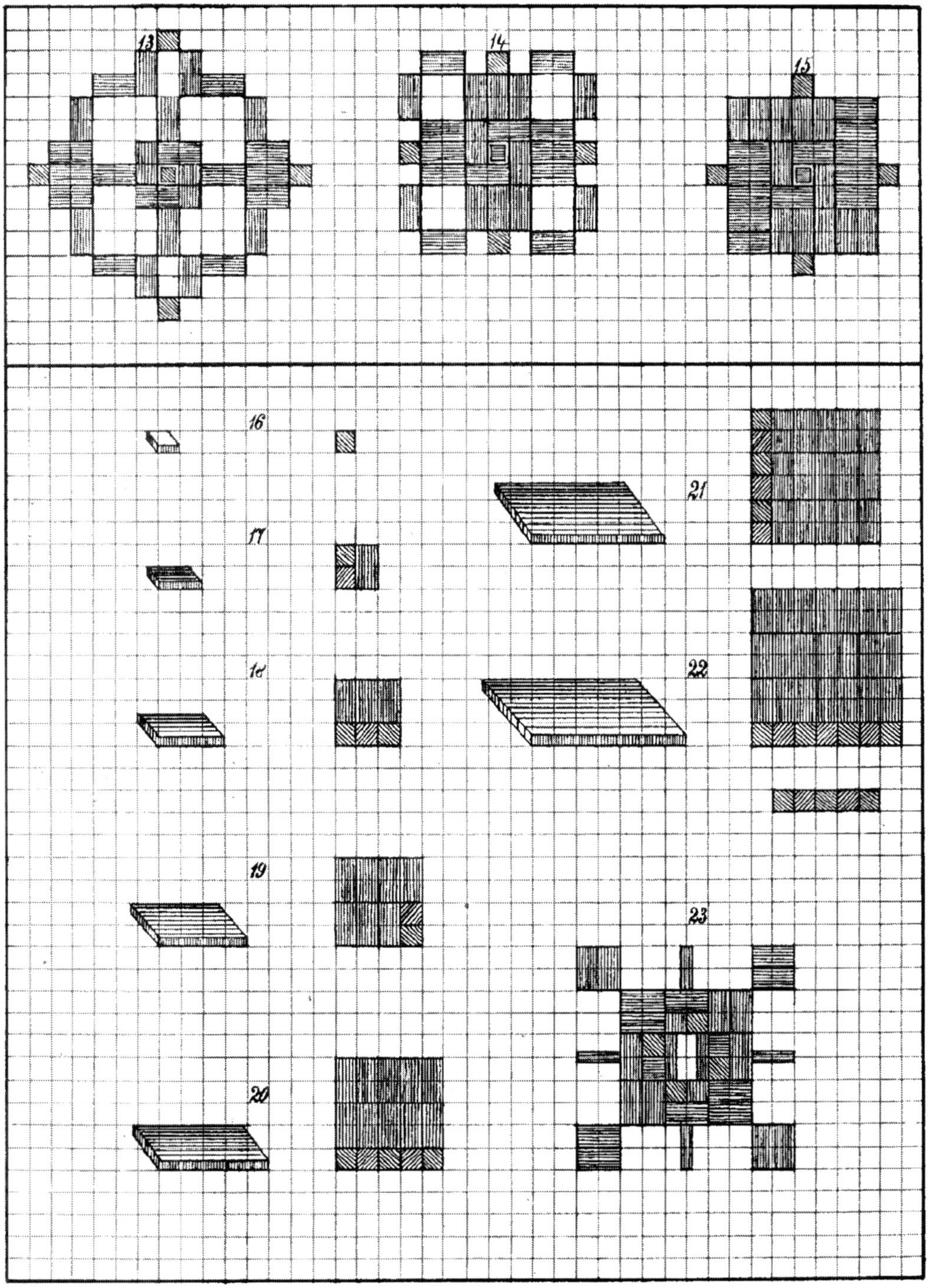
13
14
15
16
17
18
19
20
21
22
23

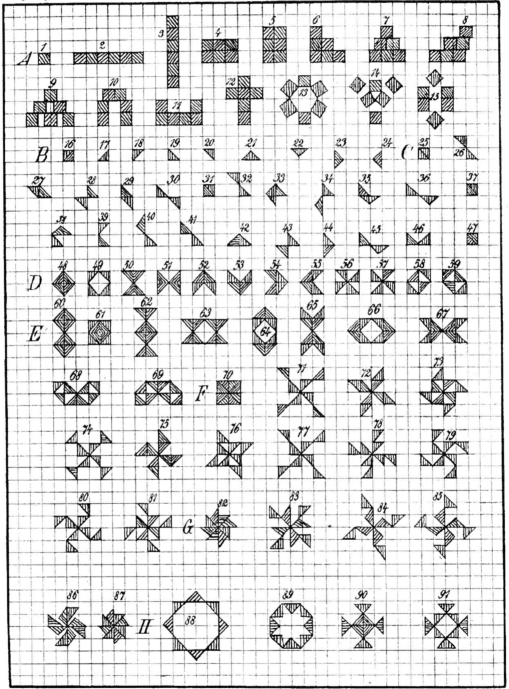

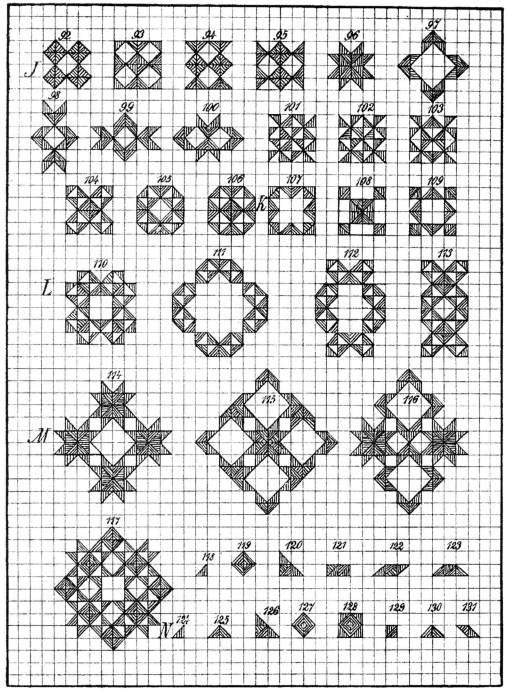

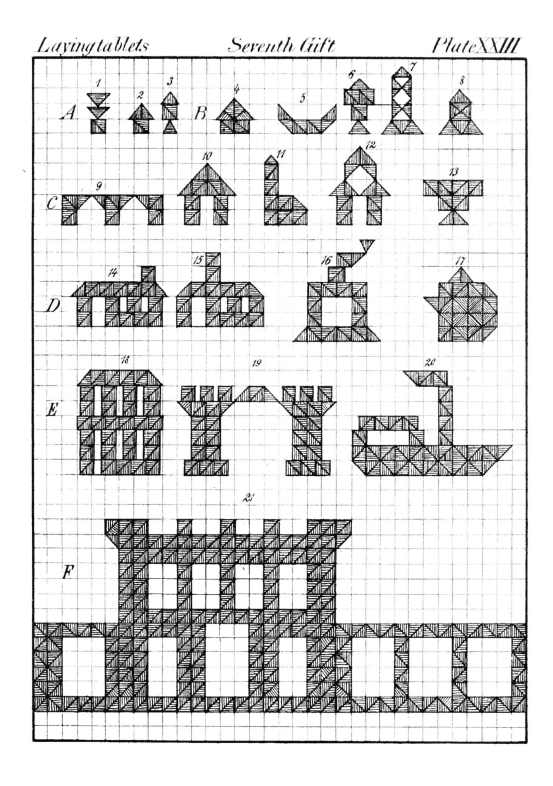

A
1
2
3
4
5
6
7
8
9
B
10
11
12
13
14
15
16
17
18
19
20
21
22
23
24
25
26
27
28
29
C
30
31
32
33
34
35
36
37
38
39
40

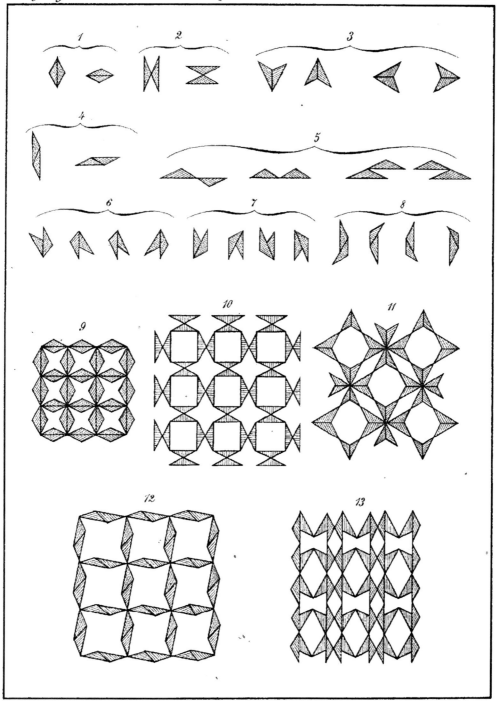

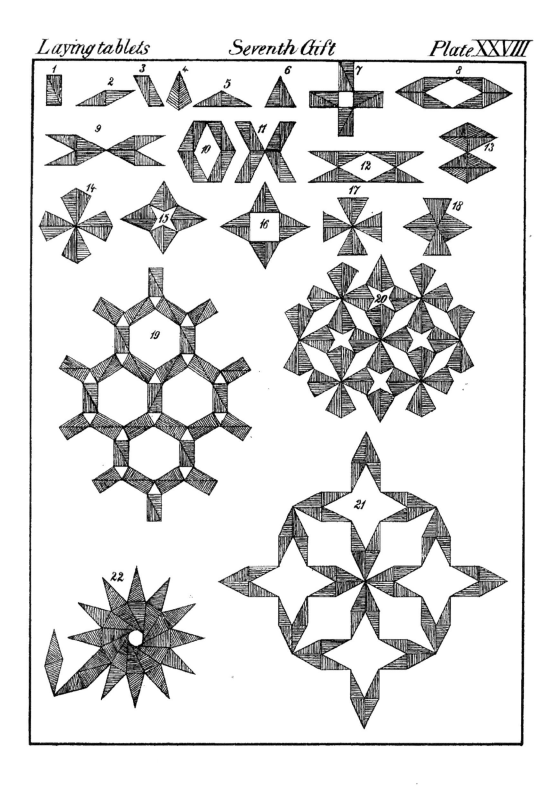

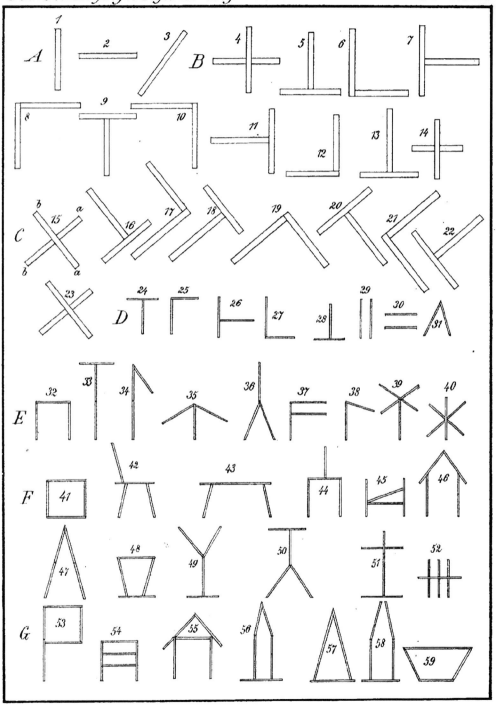

Plate XXXII

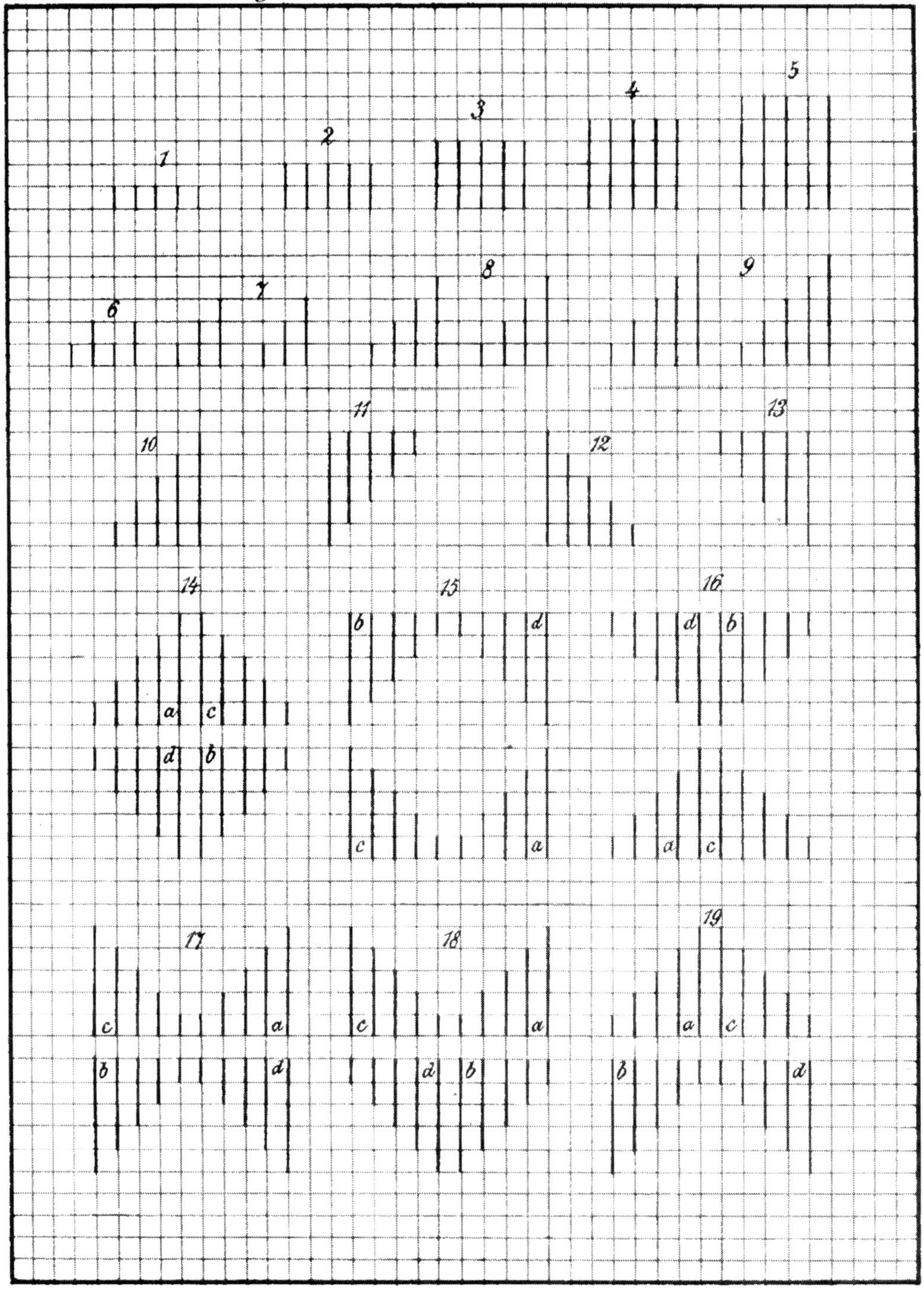
1
2
3
4
5
6
7
8
9
10
11
12
13
14
a
c
d
b
15
b
d
c
a
16
d
b
a
c
17
c
a
b
d
18
c
a
d
b
19
a
c
b
d

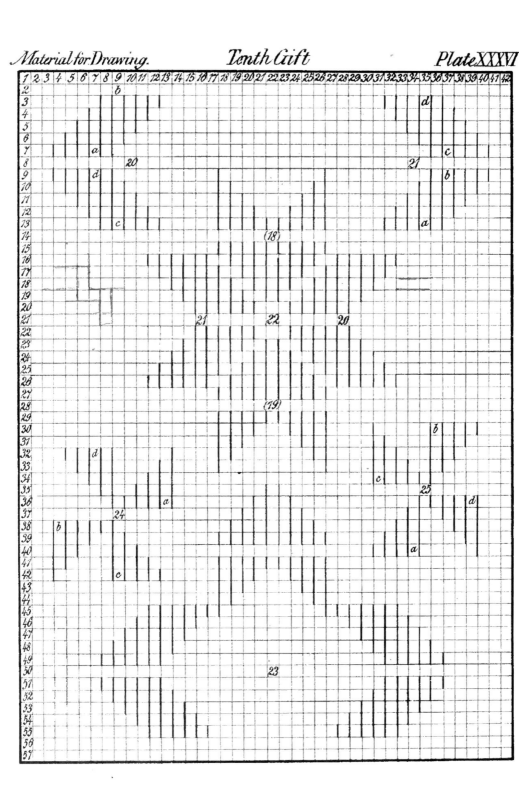

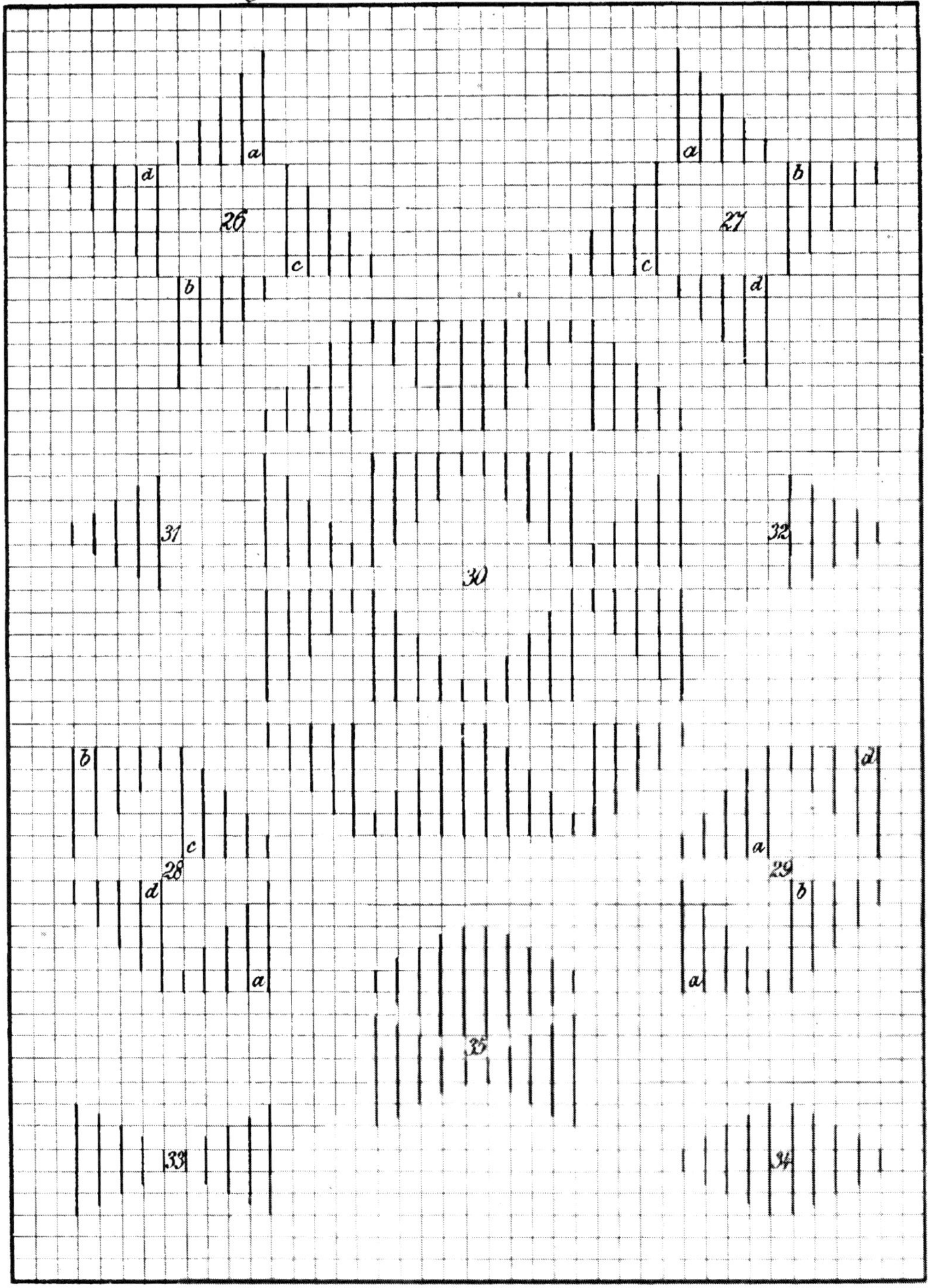
a
d
26
c
b
a
b
27
c
d
31
30
32
b
c
28
d
a
a
29
b
a
35
33
34

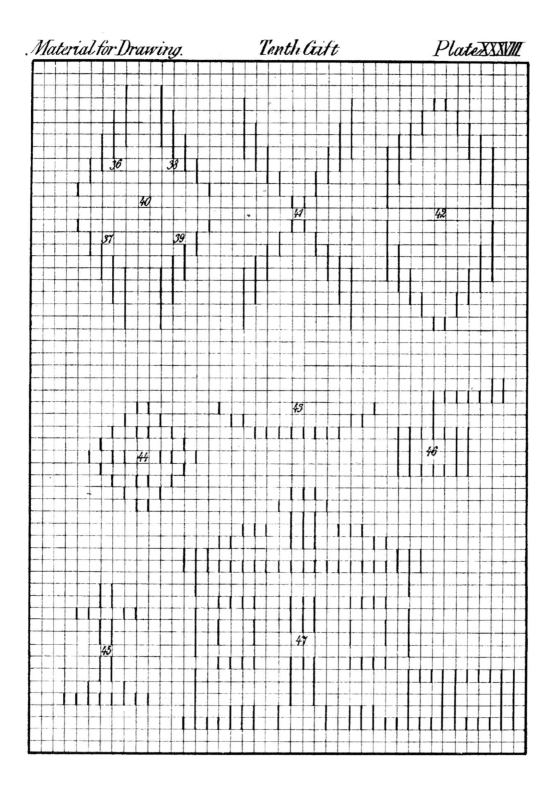

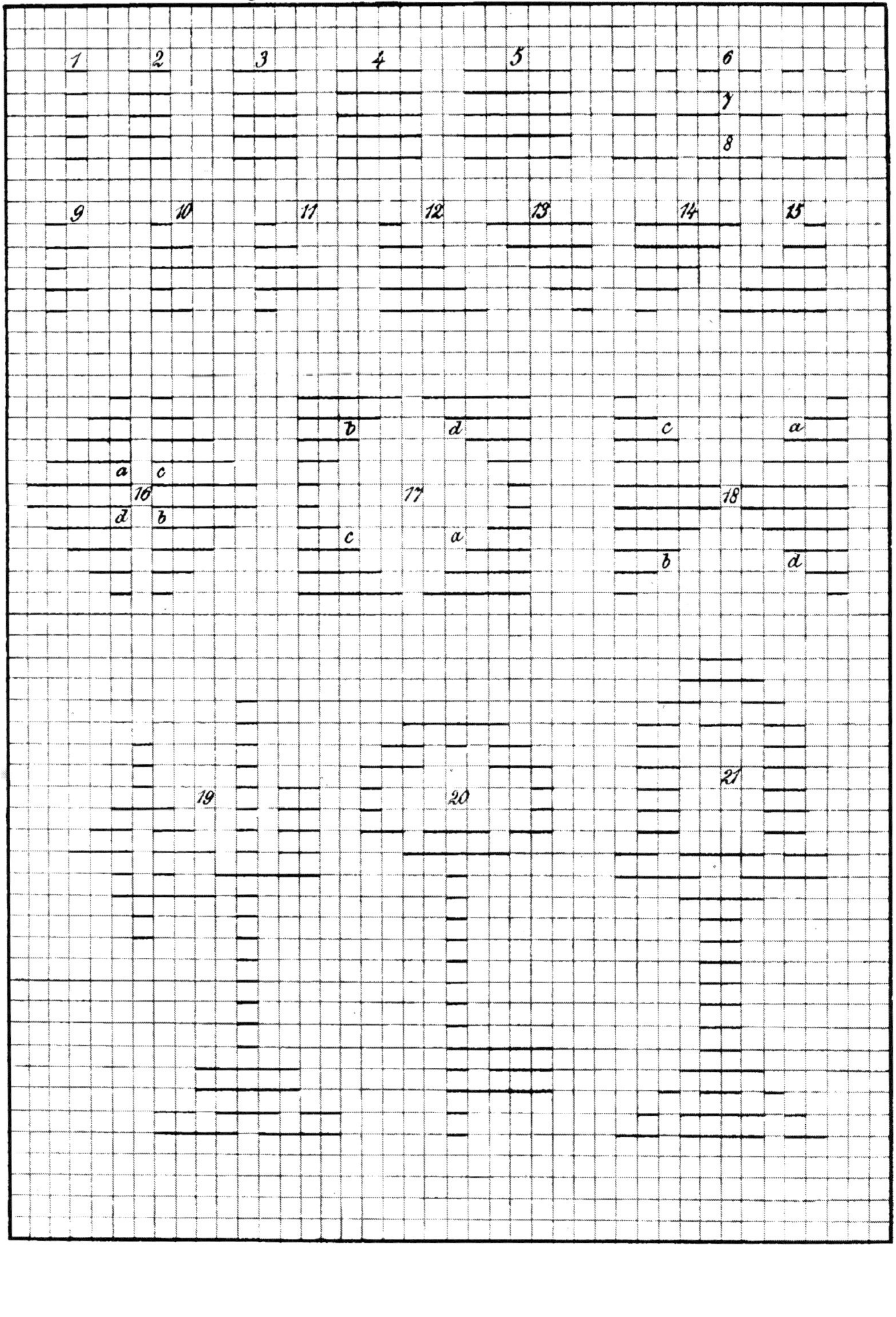
1
2
3
4
5
6
7
8
9
10
11
12
13
14
15
16
17
18
19
20
21

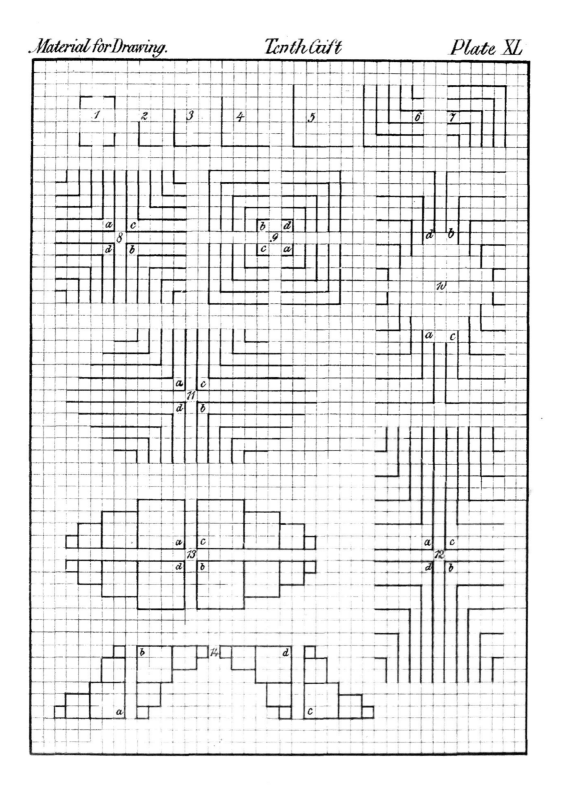

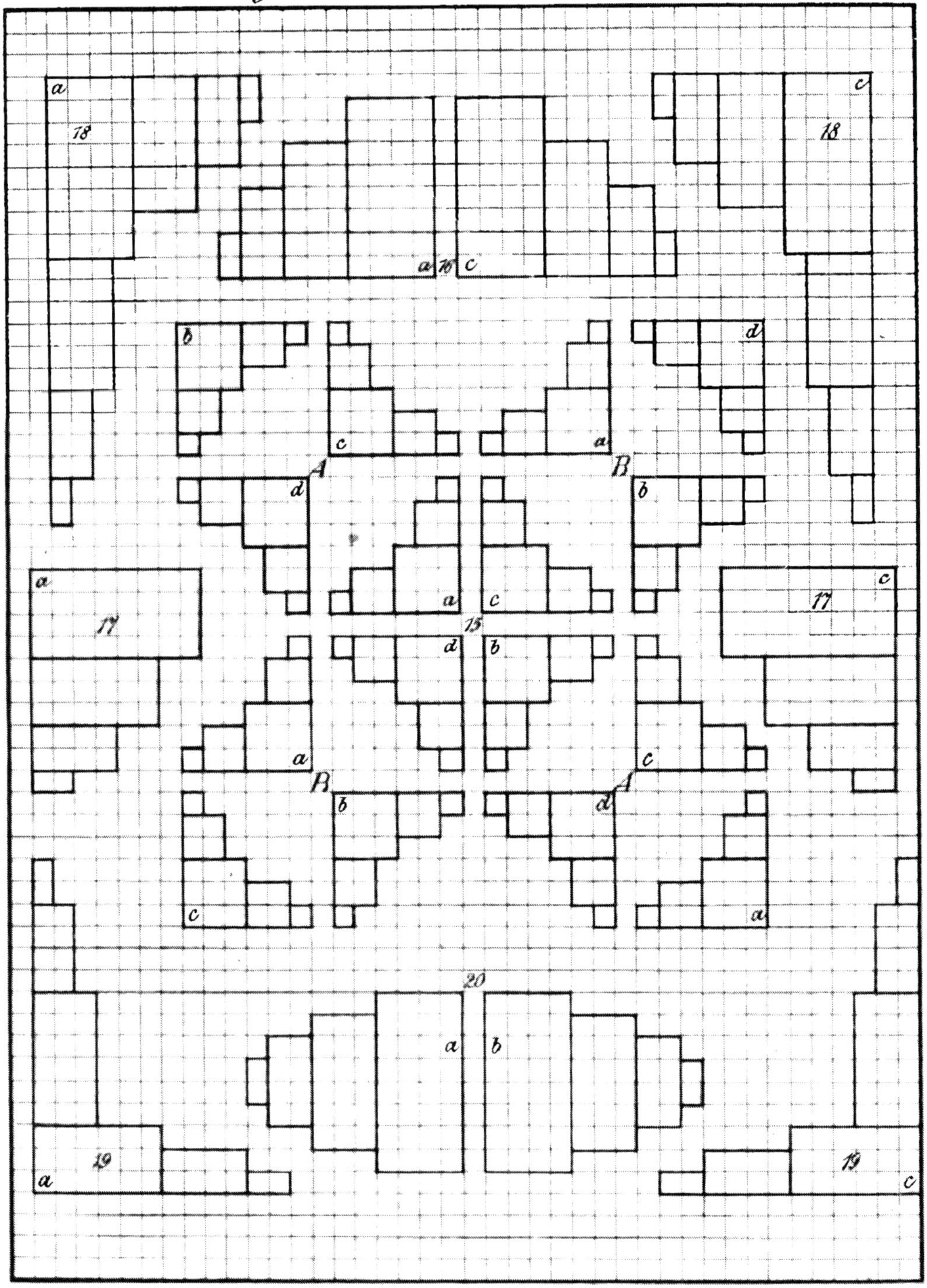
18
16
18
A
B
17
15
17
B
A
20
19
19

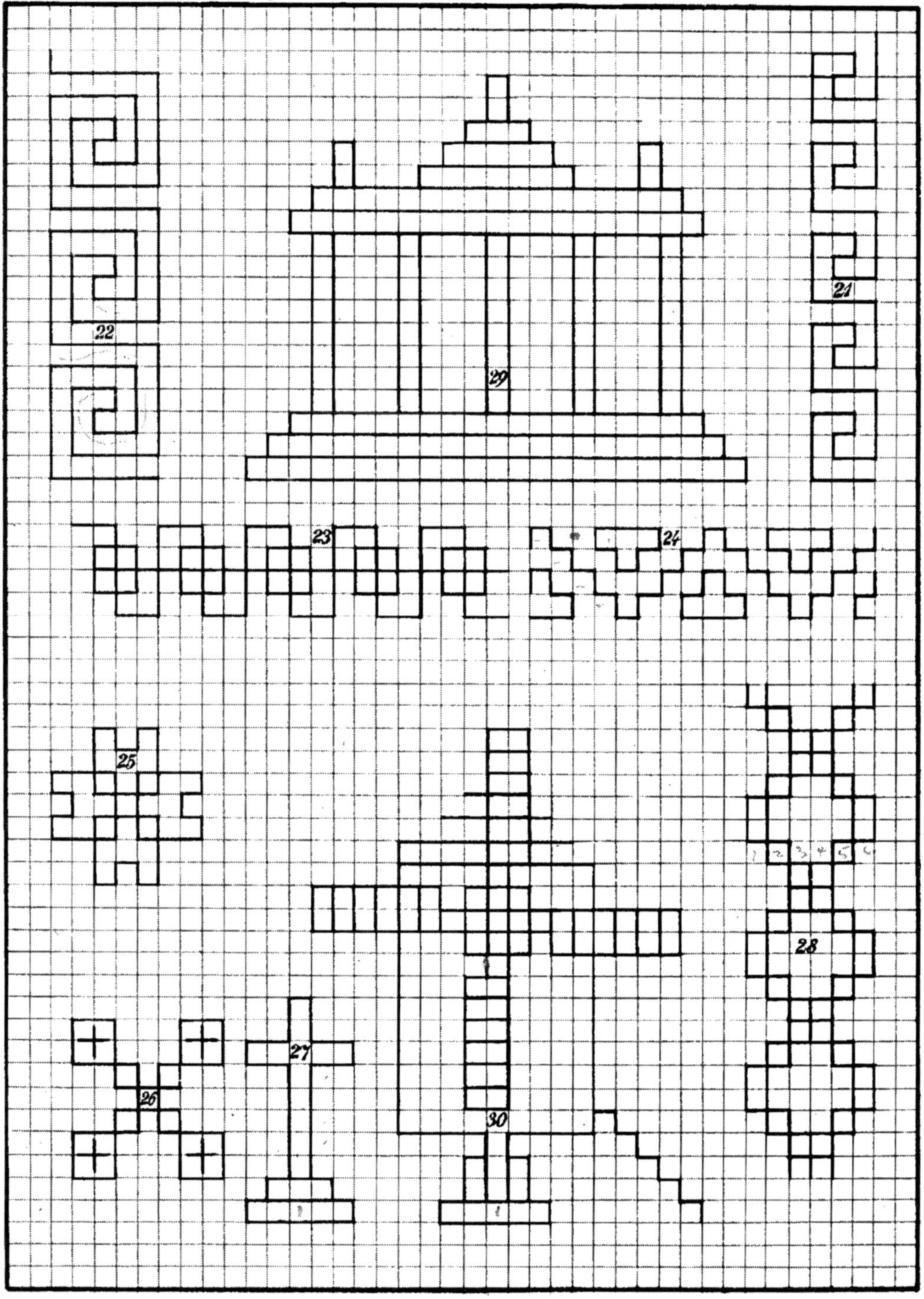
22
29
21
23
24
25
28
27
26
30

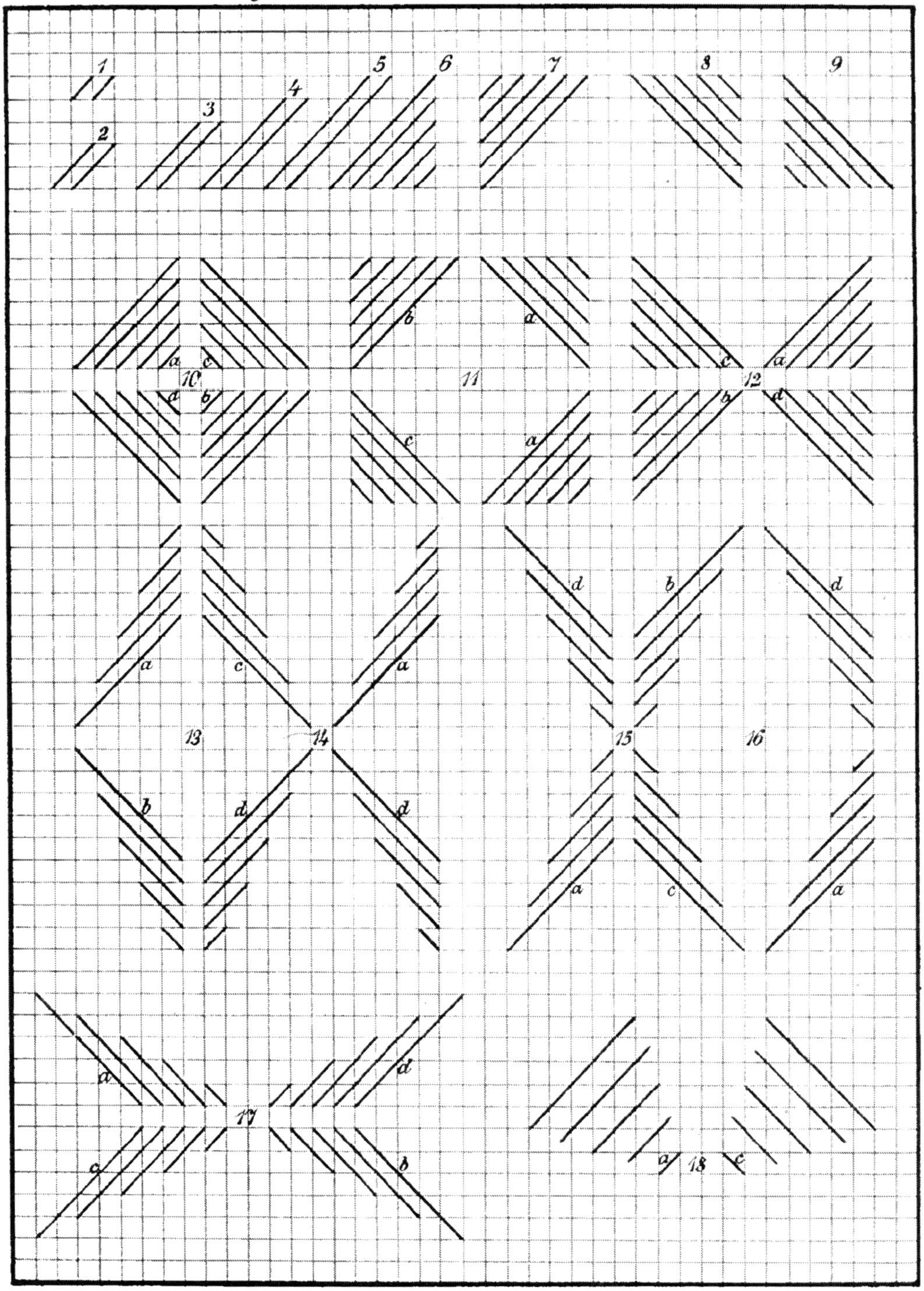
1
2
3
4
5
6
7
8
9
10
11
12
13
14
15
16
17
18
a
b
c
d

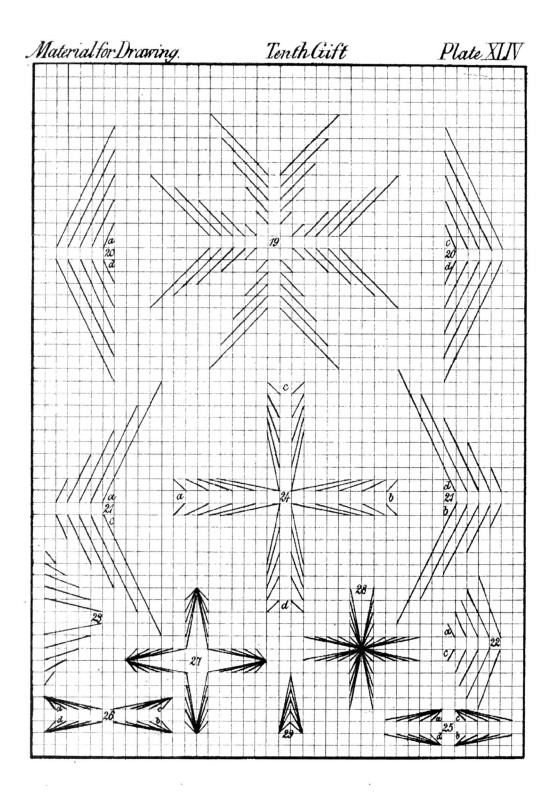

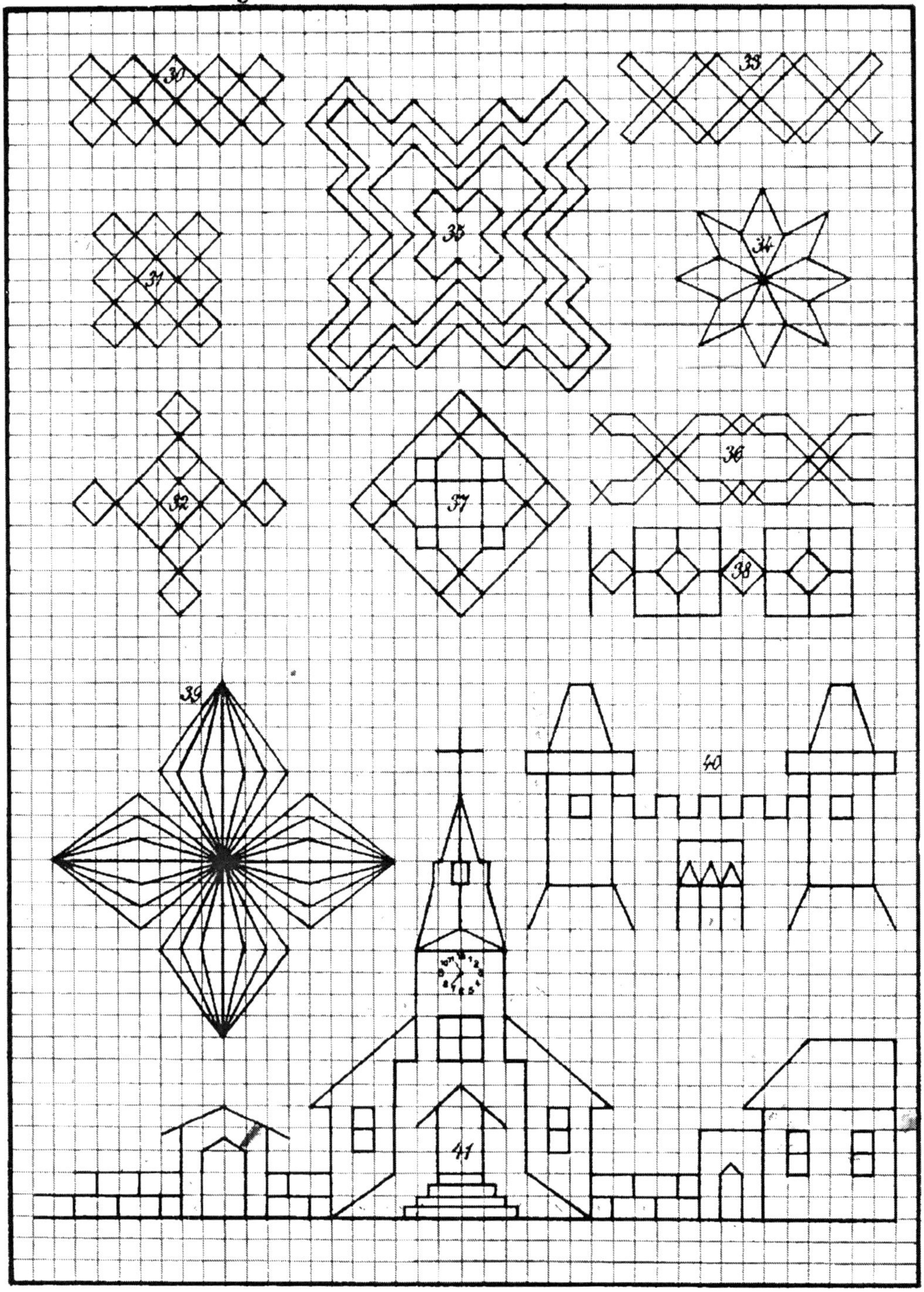
30
33
35
34
31
32
37
36
38
39
40
41

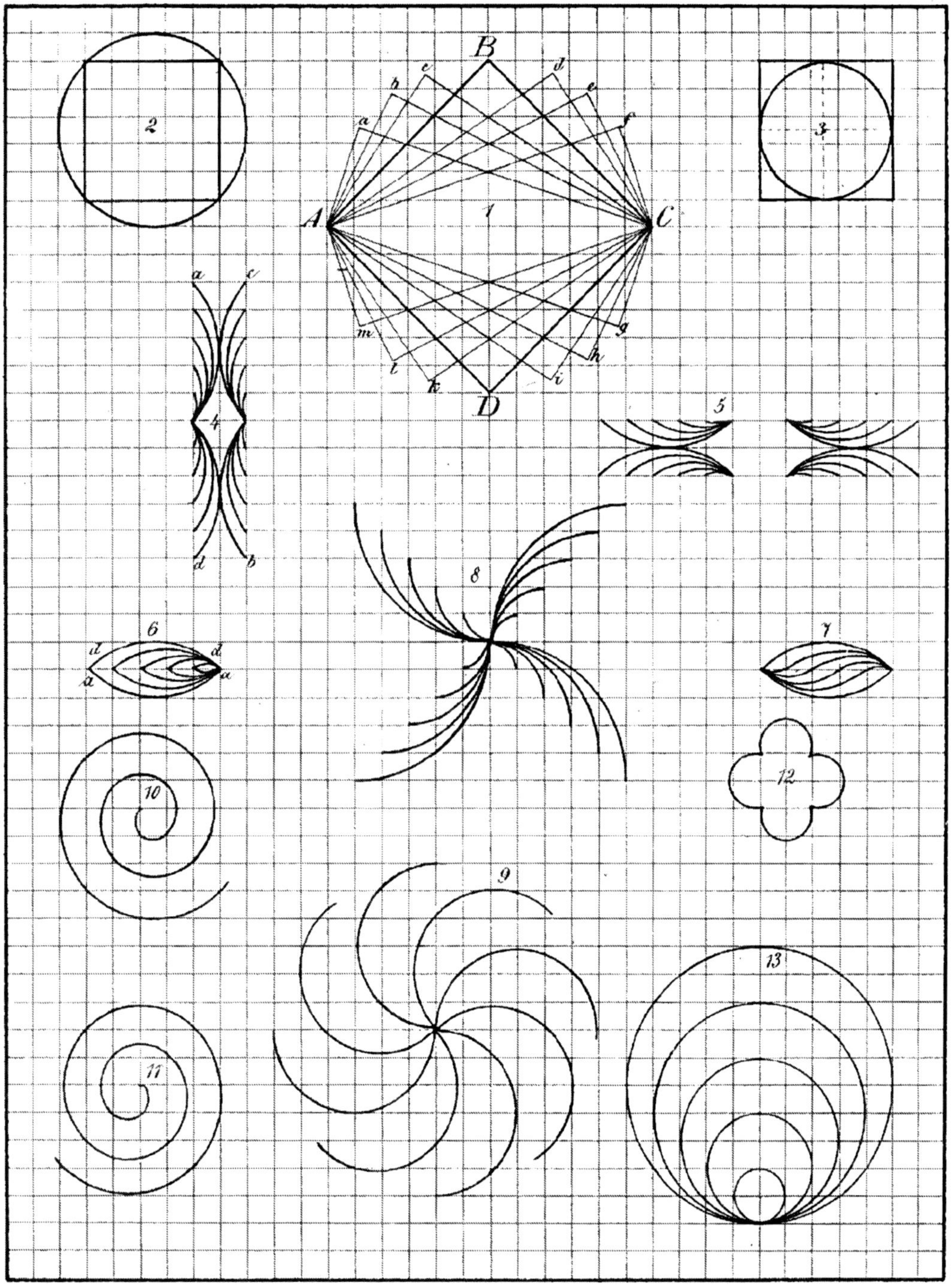
1
A
B
C
D
a
b
c
d
e
f
g
h
i
k
l
m
2
3
4
5
6
7
8
9
10
11
12
13

Material for
Perforating & Embroidering. Eleventh & Twelfth Gift Plate XLVII

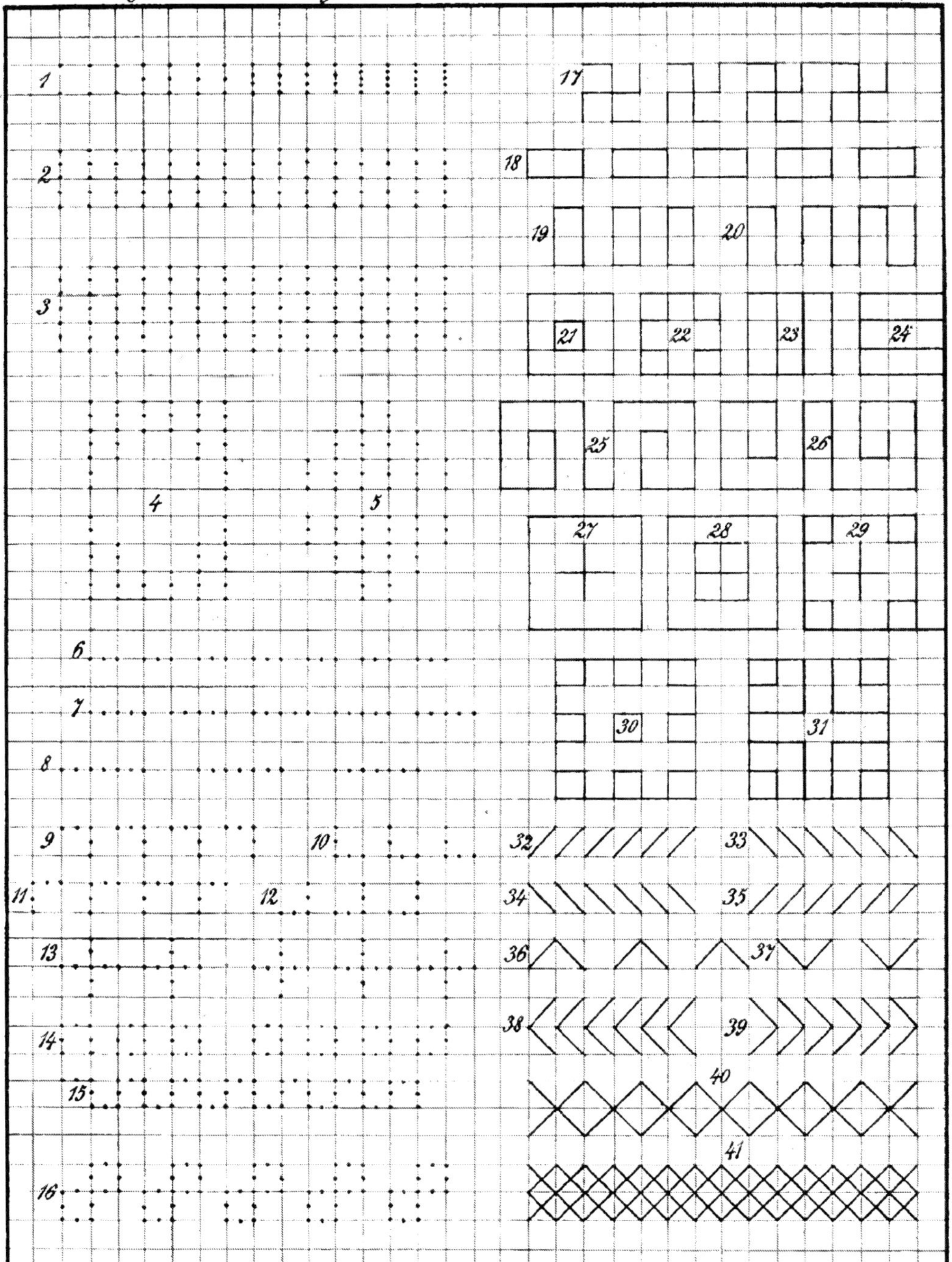

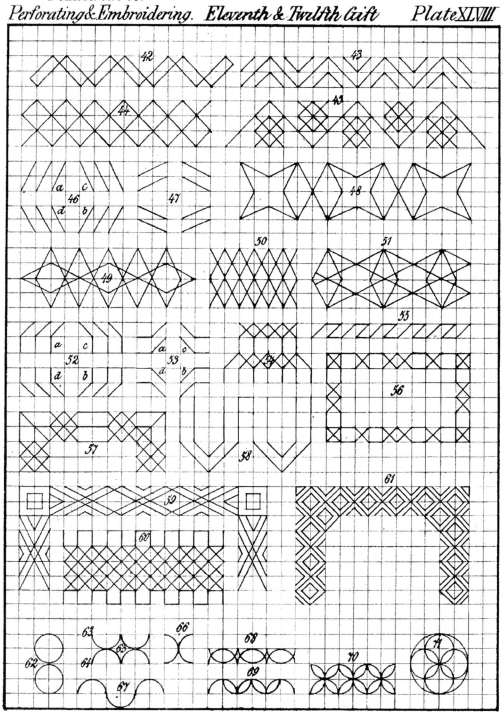

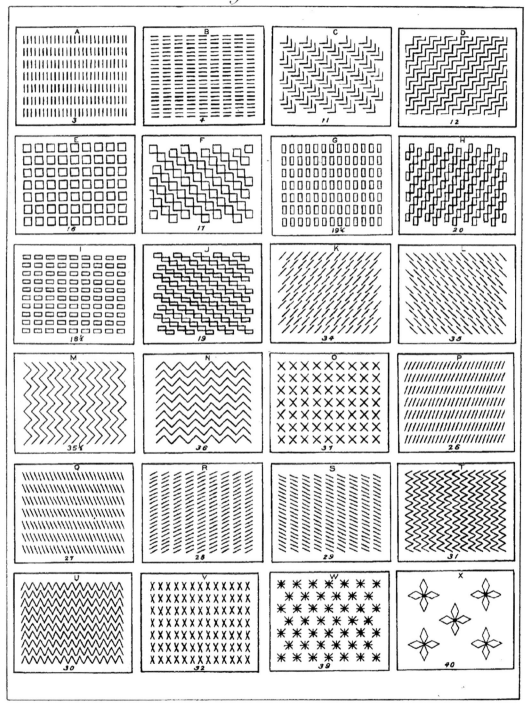

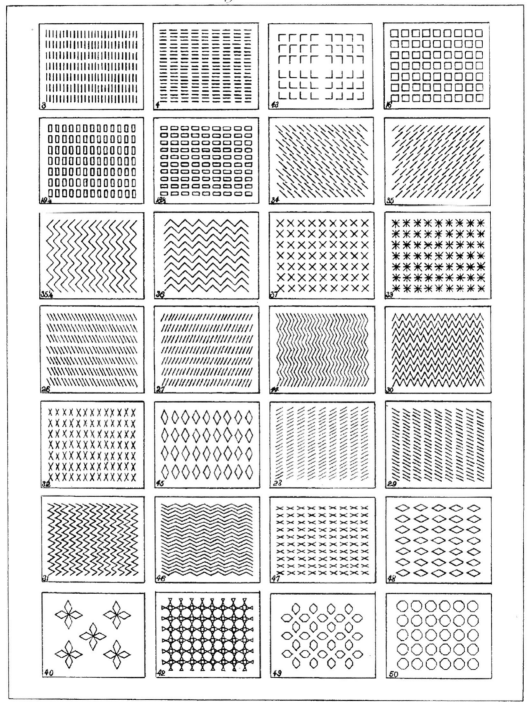

7.(№ 71)

8.(№ 82)

9.   (№ 108)

10.(№ 100)

11.(№ 124)

12.   (№ 121)

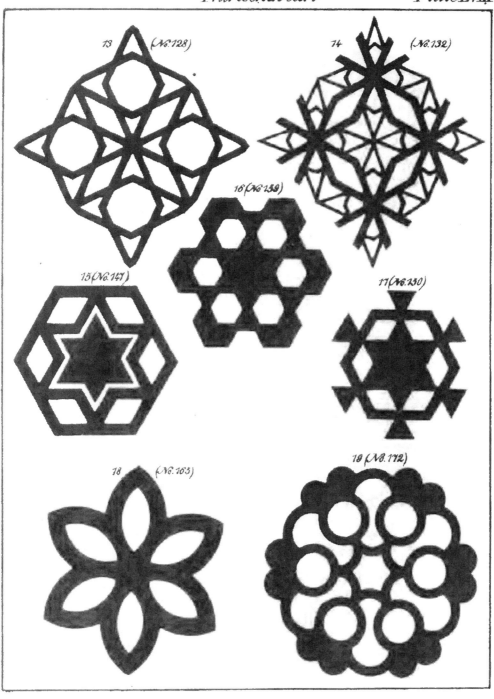

13 (No.128)
14 (No.132)
16 (No.139)
15 (No.147)
17 (No.150)
18 (No.165)
19 (No.172)

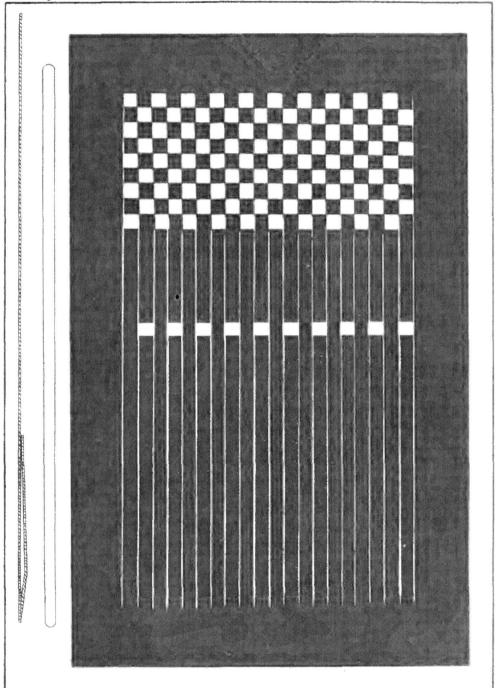

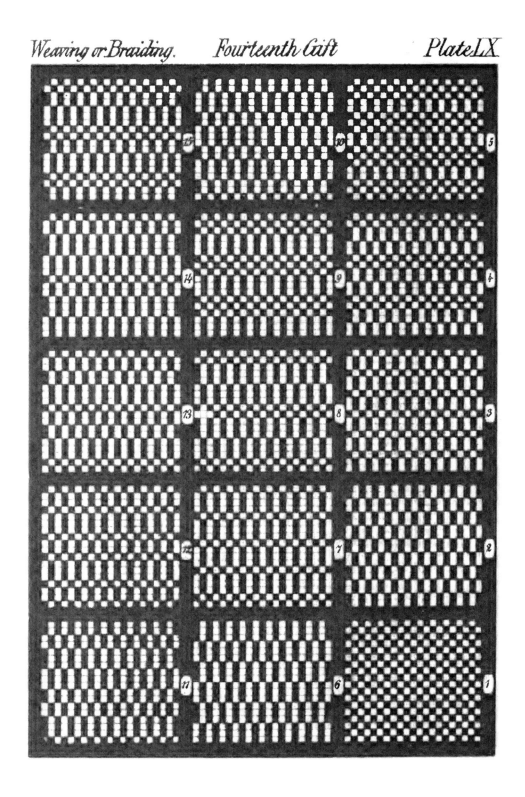

Weaving or Braiding. Fourteenth Gift Plate LXI

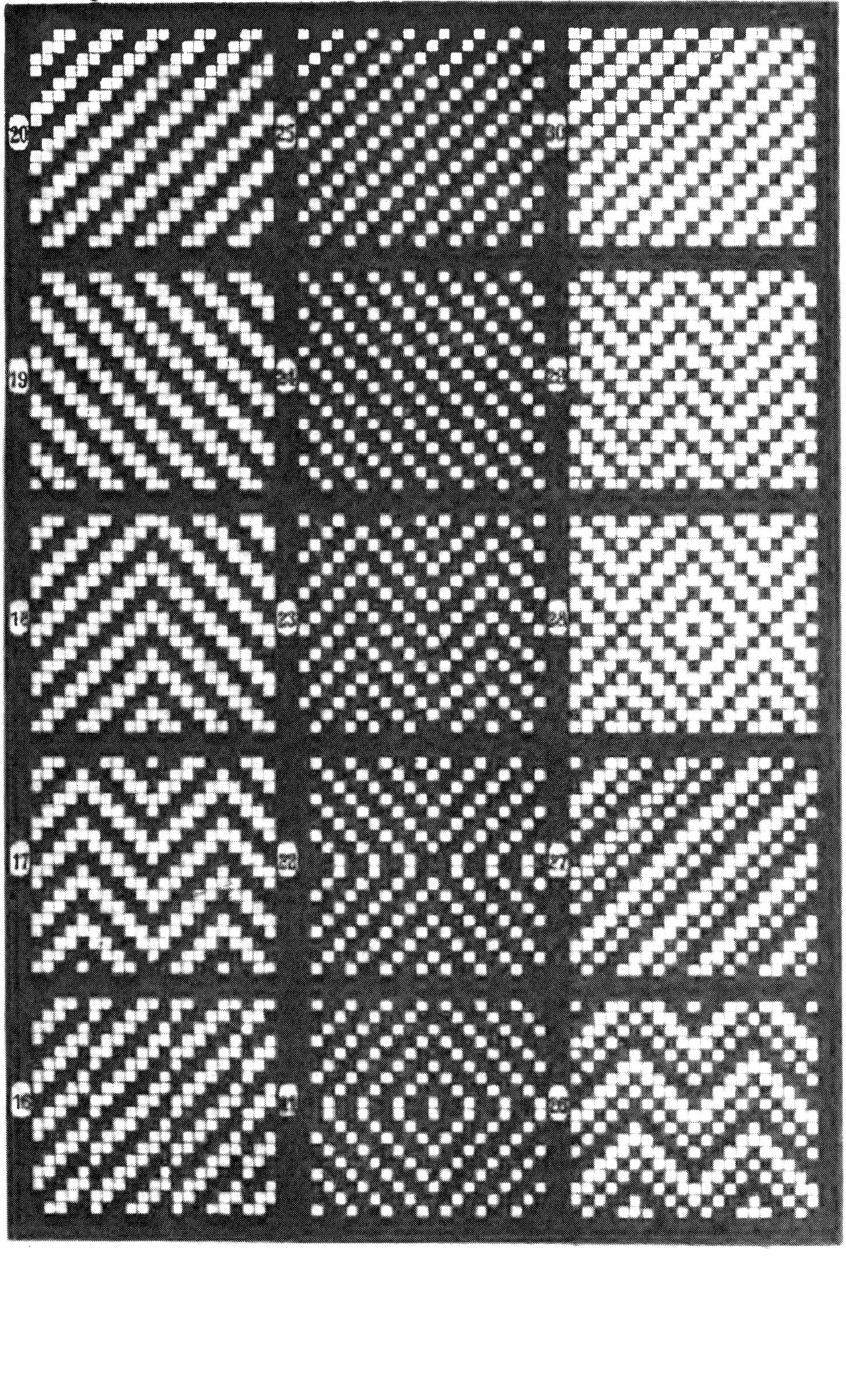

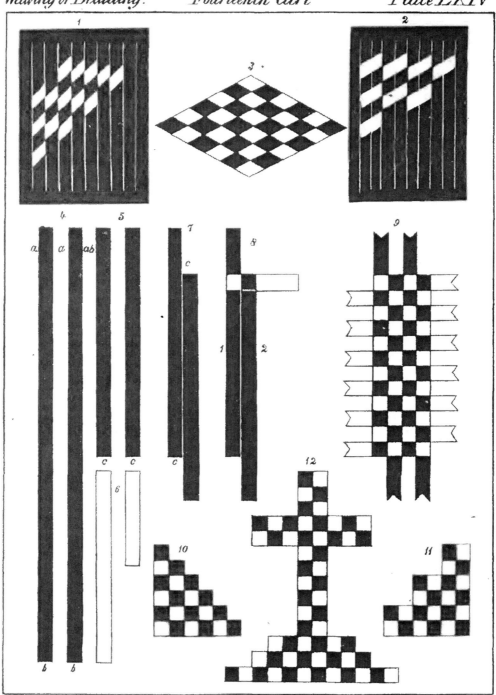

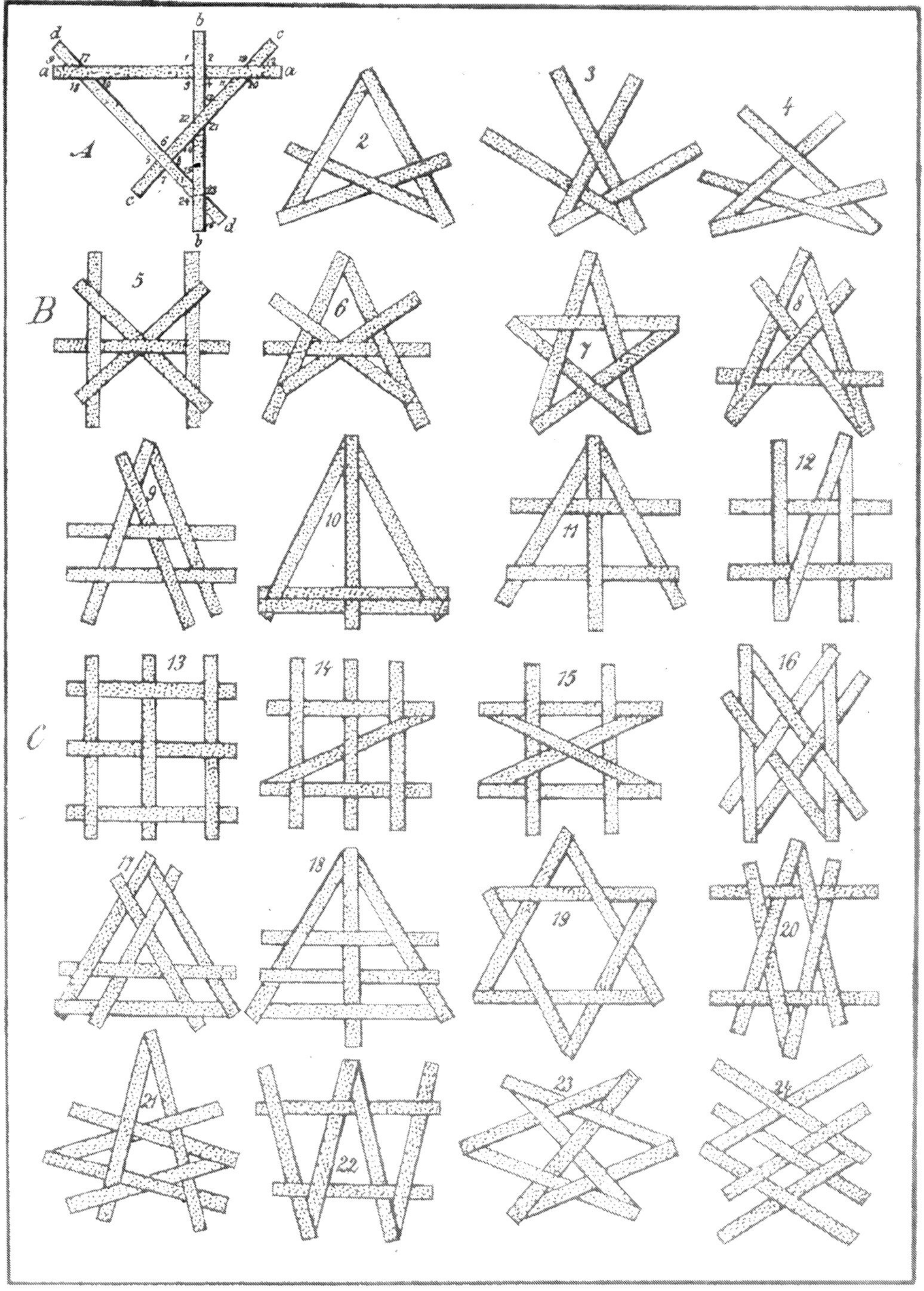
A
B
C
2
3
4
5
6
7
8
9
10
11
12
13
14
15
16
17
18
19
20
21
22
23
24

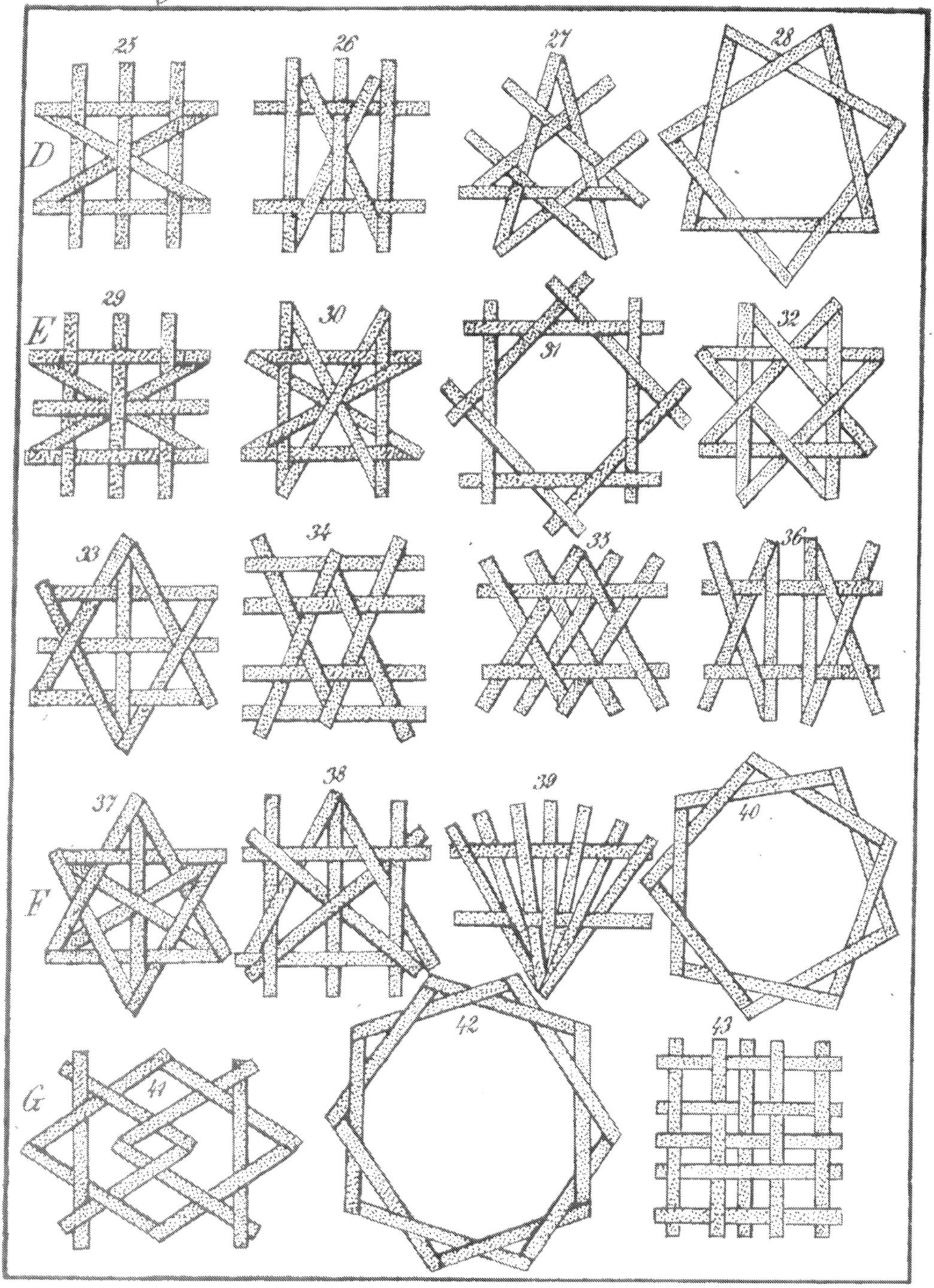
25
26
27
28
D
29
30
31
32
E
33
34
35
36
37
38
39
40
F
41
42
43
G

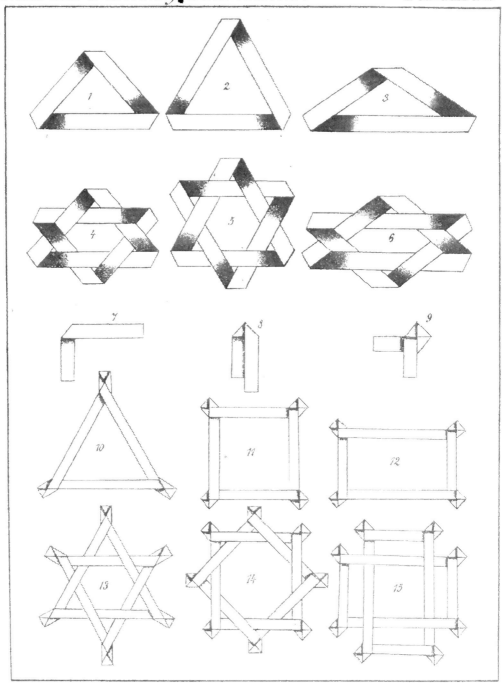

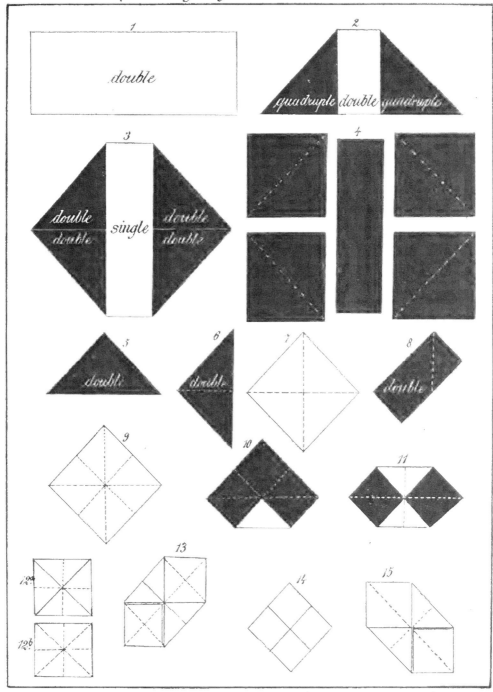

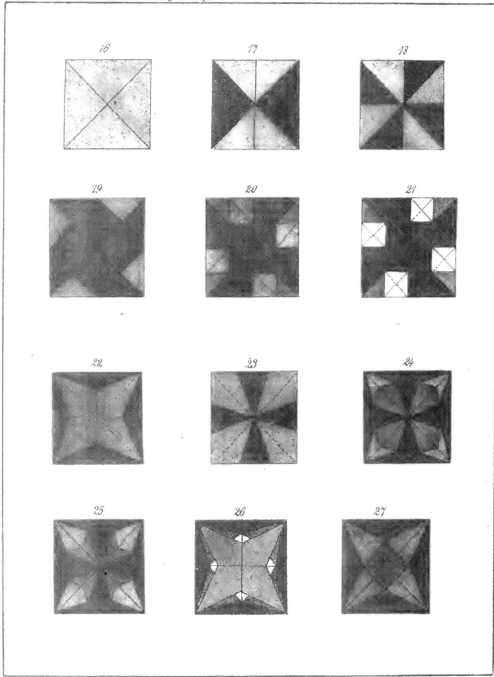

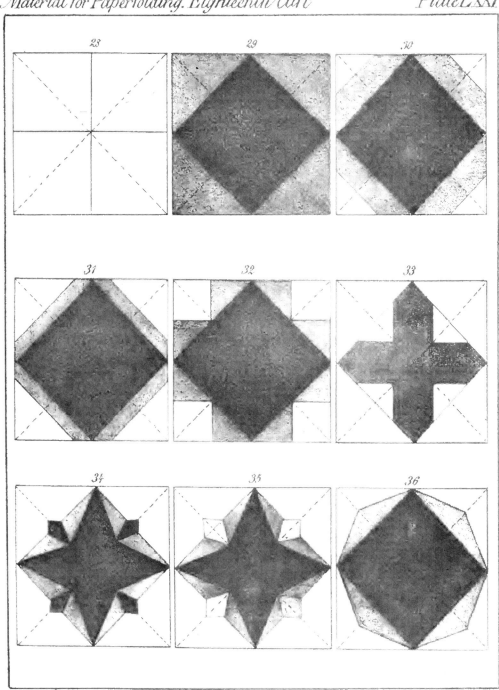

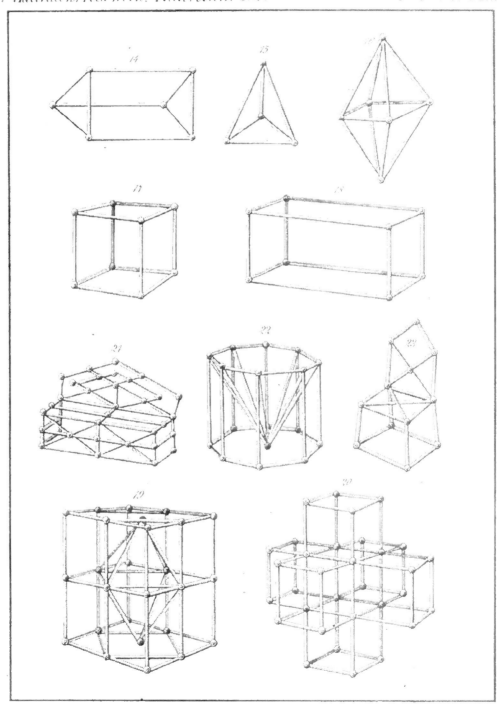

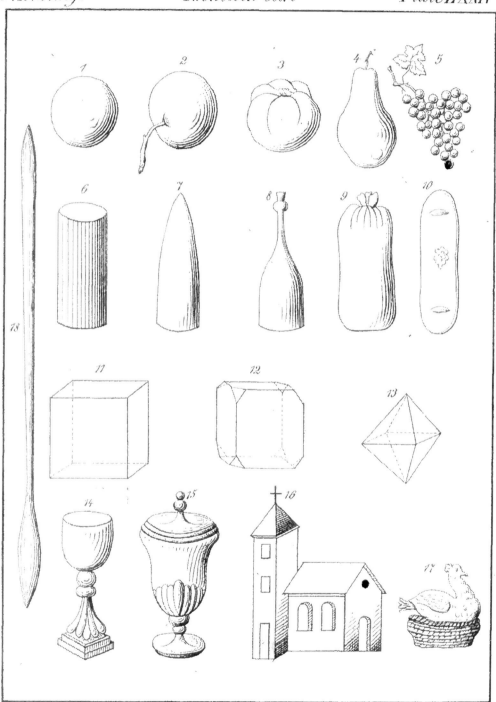

CPSIA information can be obtained at www.ICGtesting.com
Printed in the USA
LVOW11s2000220414

382766LV00014B/215/P

9 781171 611455